# And Even for This Day

# And Even For This Day

Prayers of Uneasy Allegiance to God

ANDY OLIVER

*Illustrations by Ryan Hutchison*

RESOURCE *Publications* · Eugene, Oregon

AND EVEN FOR THIS DAY
Prayers of Uneasy Allegiance to God

Resource Publications
An Imprint of Wipf and Stock Publishers
199 W. 8th Ave., Suite 3
Eugene, OR 97401

www.wipfandstock.com

PAPERBACK ISBN: 978-1-6667-1923-9
HARDCOVER ISBN: 978-1-6667-1924-6
EBOOK ISBN: 978-1-6667-1925-3

MARCH 1, 2022 1:50 PM

To the Oliver Women—Jodi, Annie Kate, Carolina—all my love

To Kim, Nick, and Morgan. Thanks for your support
and encouragement.

# Contents

# Preface

WE BELIEVE GOD IS more interesting than human beings, and we wanted prayers that brooded over a God who apparently broods over us and this planet. We wanted prayers that addressed God with our common life such that indignity and injustice were conveyed with neither the certainty such sin would be resolved nor the conviction we were on God's side of pain. We believe that at times we are the women at the cross, lamenting crucifixion, and at other times we are the empire's minions banging in the nails. This is where we find ourselves, sometimes victimized and sometimes enacting betrayal, always within the earshot of our enemy's creator.

We believe that human expression towards God and towards each other transcends words. We also believe that the human experience could be more expansively carried through images. Thus, we have interwoven some of our paintings throughout the written words.

These prayers were offered to God on behalf of a worshipping congregation. Thus, they include the names of our dead and sometimes the specifics of our common life. If you are part of a worshipping community, perhaps you can use parts of these prayers in your services. When we prayed these prayers in our worship services they were usually followed by the Lord's Prayer.

Prayer is a two-way event, a conversation. The Jewish prophets were gifted (or cursed) with conveying the needs and desires of both God and humans to each other. Popular spirituality focuses on being silent before God. We get it. Humans generally talk too much. And yet Scripture is filled with the attempt by humans to trust God with their lives through speech. We follow in the footsteps of Jesus, who instructed his followers to pray . . . using words.

Finally, we recognize that there are many reasons a person may find it difficult to engage the church. A deep ambivalence as to the way the church talks to God is one of them. Our hope is that those on the edges of Christian community might overhear the possibility of honest speech and want to join in.

## A BEGINNING*

Gracious God, we thank you for your love. We are here because of it, whether we can recognize it or not. Whether we can give your love a name or not. Whether we love you back or not, whether we can glorify you because of it or not . . . nevertheless . . . we are here because of your love.

Perhaps, Dear Christ, that is your favorite word, not love but *nevertheless*. Nevertheless is the word that carries us from death to life, as in on a Friday Jesus died nevertheless he 'rose' up on a Sunday.

Hospitable Holy Spirit, nevertheless carries us from fear to joy, as in when my loved one died I was afraid . . . nevertheless . . . God held me. Nevertheless is that hinge word between our fear and your grace.

Gracious God, you do a lot of mischief with a word, and in a word, and through a word like "nevertheless". It's like your pause button. In that pause, you travel to whatever hells we are found, either of our own making or the making of others, and you climb down into them and whisper, "This is not where you need to be. You could be free—you could be in love."

Rescuing Spirit, you stalk the halls of hospitals, the loneliness of dinners for one, the numbness of pixels, the tear gas of protests, the heartbreak of parenthood, the anger of injustice and you say, "Nevertheless . . . I love you and you were born for me."

Sustaining God, for your flesh and blood Nevertheless that is Jesus the Christ, we pray as he taught us praying . . .

* Prayer inspired by Walter Brueggemann's writings.

## A CURT NOD

Almighty God, with what do we come before you and bow ourselves within your grace? You are pleased with us, because you called us into life, not out of your need but out of your desire.

For you need us like you need a giraffe or a panda or a slug. That is, you do not need us, you simply wanted us. On behalf of giraffes, pandas, and slugs everywhere, and the plants upon which they feed, and the earth's crust upon which it all rests, we thank you.

Gracious God, with what do we come before you to bow ourselves to your royal holiness or at least offer a curt nod of deference in your indeterminate direction, or is it acknowledgement of your possible bland existence, or is it some cultural habit from another generation's childhood? Regardless we came this day, so . . . you're welcome.

Creating God, with what do we come before you? Will you be pleased with our fluttering and flittering, our shuffling of papers and keeping of schedules, our obsession with security, and if not getting ahead at least holding our own, keeping our own, pushing away those who threaten our own, our heads bowed down to our screens?

Sustaining God, with what do we come before you? We have tried to get close to you, but with heavy heads hanging down and scoliotic spines turned inwards to our own altars of depression or sickness or pain, we do not know if we will be welcomed.

You will have to lift our faces for us. We do not have the desire nor the memory of your mercy to do so on our own. Amen.

## A LIFE TOO SMALL

Gracious God, we thank you for the gift of life. The gift of salvation. Salvation from fear, salvation from sin, salvation from timidity, salvation from being too casual and chatty with you.

You hold the mystery of sin and death, you keep the waters of the deep at bay, you hold the glory of all nations, you wield the keys to heaven and hell.

And we . . . well we have anxiety. We worry and fret about money, and possessions, and the advancement of our children. And whether our arthritic knee will stop aching. And the neighbor's dog, Lord how we worry about the inconveniences of our neighbors.

Forgive us when we live a life too small for you. Do not forgive us our silence but do forgive us when we fail to ally ourselves with the voiceless.

Do not forgive us our wonderment but do forgive us when we are no longer in awe of your creation, when we treat your earth with such contempt.

Do not forgive us our desire for safety but do forgive us when we kill on its behalf.

Do not forgive us our need to work and find meaning in our labor but do forgive us when we waver at the injustices of financial exploitation.

For you God, are also the giver of life, the reconciler of rupture, you are not our guard, rather you are our lover. Your ways are not our ways, for your way is the Jesus way And we pray as Jesus taught us, praying . . .

## A LONG MEMORY

Holy and Merciful God, we thank thee for your heart of justice, a long memory for the orphan and widow, and even for this day.

Gracious God, we lament the death of Brianna Taylor—and how can it ever be right for men to burst into her apartment at night and shoot her six times to death for doing nothing more than being in her apartment at night, terrified, and everybody else walks away like nothing has happened. We will never understand the ways of men.

God who keeps our memories, we may be the richest nation, but let us not call ourselves a Christian one. You, Jesus, would never slap your moniker on these kinds of behaviors.

God with a long memory for the orphan and widow, if goodness and righteousness and forgiveness and reconciliation will not come and settle upon our nights, let us at least see it coming on the morning horizon.

Jesus, please come . . .

Oh God who has taken the very stinger out of death, we lift up to you Lois and Jan. Before they were ours, they are yours. As in, they still belong to you even though they no longer belong to us.

Jesus our Shepherd, comfort us in our grief until that day when we shall all be brought together to sit down upon the wet green grass while Peter and Bartholomew shovel out all-you-can-eat bread and fish, and we are laughing and saying out loud, "Thanks and thanks again." And "What was that all about?" And "Here, you go first." And "Let me hold the door for you." And "I love you." And "Isn't it grand . . . isn't God all grand!"

In the name of the one who holds our memory we pray . . .

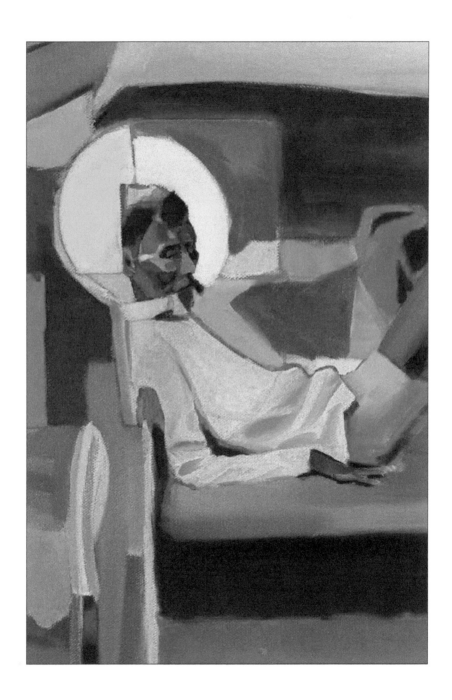

## ADDING LETTERS

Holy and Merciful God, we thank thee for life and limb, for love and liberation as we approach our worship of you this day.

LGBTQIAP + . . . Dear God, we keep adding letters and losing churches. And both the letters and the churches represent people—are people—are our brothers and sisters in Christ. The same ones we now move to separate from after you have given your life to join together.

We pray for the freedom to include fully into church life and leadership folks who are gay or queer or trans or who are attempting to figure out gender and personhood in this wacked out, beautiful, dangerous world.

May we, by your grace, be the kind of church where all can belong while we figure out how to be. For we do not know who we are without the offensive presence of our neighbors.

We pray for those who have been murdered or assaulted or have engaged in self-harm or have died by suicide because they have been mis-gendered or misassigned or mismanaged or mis-cared for—because they were gay or queer or trans or otherwise who dared to live outside the suffocation of loveless power. You, Oh Christ, have lived their life, died their death, and you are the first fruit of their resurrection.

We also pray for those who are torn asunder by tradition, who did nothing wrong except grow up never knowing there was something besides male and female. We pray for the uncertain, the uncomfortable, those who want to go slower, those who do not want to be seen as judgmental and yet are given no space to ponder and think without being mis-assigned as judgmental. You, Oh Christ, have lived their life, died their death, and you are the first fruit of their resurrection.

We also pray for those who believe anything outside of what has gone before is a sin. Those who believe if it was good enough for our parents and grandparents, it must be good. For those who believe God ordained only three categories (male, female, and heterosexual) and are tired of it all. You,

Oh Christ, have lived their life, died their death, and you are the first fruit of their resurrection.

Forgive us when our church politics are no different from the politics outside our church. Forgive us when our witness of reconciliation only comes with divorce. May we show the world how to be friends with those who voted against us.

And most of all we pray for the poor, who are often missing from this fight and yet are never missing from your gaze.

We seek the power of the Holy Spirit through the prayer Jesus taught us to pray . . .

## ADVENT

Wondrous Messiah, King of Kings, Lord of Lords and all the rest of it. We don't know for sure, but this year it seems like a John the Baptist kind of Christmas. For the year we and the world have had, maybe only a monastic screed in the wilderness will do, something with a little camel hair on it.

Prince of peace, perhaps we should just skip the manger, magi, and Bethlehem star and stay with the locust-eating, wild eyed, spittle-soaked lover . . . Johnny-in-the-desert, baptizer of your Son, seeker of repentance, proclaimer of prophecy.

By your power, let us dispatch nostalgia. It distracted but in the end was never powerful enough to dispatch death. We were never all that powerful. Perhaps that's why COVID and quarantine are so hard, it forces us to notice.

Father and Mother of us all, you send John the Baptist to proclaim our need for repentance. He said, "Repent, For the Kingdom of God is at hand!" You told him to say it.

Of what do we need to repent? It was a hard year and we could think of a few things we would like others to repent of . . . but what should we repent over?

Does Jesus's coming depend upon our repentance, or does the birth happen without our participation? Does our refusal banish us to disappear like a mouth behind a mask?

Dear God, what do we need to shed and jettison and leave behind in order to come to the manger? We have a few suggestions we would like to make on behalf of our enemies, but as for us . . .

O Holy Spirit, you are the baptism by fire, what must you burn before we can walk as children of the light? How must we catch fire to follow the Christ child?

You tell us and maybe the Kingdom will arrive.

In the name of the Child we must follow we pray . . .

## ALL SAINT'S DAY

Holy and Merciful God, we thank thee for your love, for life, and even for this day.

Dear God, this All Saints' Sunday, we thank you for the saints of biblical faith, the saints of the church, and the saints in our lives without whom we would not be in this sanctuary today.

Dear God, we are thankful for the saints of the Bible, we are thankful for Mary, the Mother of Jesus, who said yes to your salvation.

We are thankful for the unnamed bent over woman whose devotion to you taught us faithful resilience.

We are thankful for Dorcas who taught us that faith without works of mercy and justice is dead.

We thank you for the gospel writers Matthew, Mark, Luke, and John.

Dear God, we are especially thankful of the murderer Moses, the fornicator and adulterer and murderer Kind David, the prostitute Rahab, the thief and liar Jacob, the accessory to murder the Apostle Paul, the idolater Aaron, and the many other breakers of the Ten Commandments who were also carriers of your salvation and without whom we would not be a Christian church.

Dear God, we thank you for the saints of the church, the murderer King Henry the VIII, Susanna Wesley, John and Charles Wesley, Menno Simons, Francis Asbury, Mary McLeod Bethune, Anna Howard Shaw, Oscar Romero, and countless others whose mix of faith and failure have been caught up to your glory.

Dear God, it is not their perfection by which imperfect people are made into your people, but rather by your mercy.

And now we publicly name those who have pushed us, cajoled us, enticed us, and basically loved us into following your Son. Who are the others that need to be named right now . . . ?

Dear God, for their faith and witness we are able to pray as Jesus taught us to pray . . .

## AND STILL WE DIE

Holy and Merciful God we thank thee for life and love and even for this day.

Creator, Father, and Mother of all your children across all your world . . . What are we to make of the news today that we have killed another terrorist leader? How do we carry to you our relief or at least resigned complacency that a murderer has been murdered?

What, Jesus, would you do? You, oh Crucified and Risen One. You who did not spare your followers from their own violent death, what would you do with a terrorist? With a man committed to murder who at the same time was somebody's child, somebody's son, somebody's brother. Not ours of course, but somebody's.

We know, oh Crucified and Risen One, that you would not kill nor ask your followers to do the same. For that commandment has been enshrined in your Holy Word. So how, oh God of life and death, do we give you our desires to live a life free from terror?

Dear Holy Spirit who breathes life into existence and without whom we would not be, we pray for your protection from violence even as we deny the Prince of Peace by our acts of violence. Dear Savior, we use violence to save ourselves, to establish peace, not unlike the Romans who killed you.

And still we die, just like the ones we kill. Oh God of life and death, in the end we all die no matter how many we kill. How then O Prince of Peace, are we to live until we die in you?

We pray as Jesus taught us to pray . . .

## ANIMATED PRAISE

Creator God, you originated with life. Redeemer God, your starting point is salvation. Sanctifying God, you begin with gift. Your first exhale was love. Your first word brought light. The first sweep of your big toe kicked the world into existence. You reached down into the deep; the muck and mire and mud and spit, and you quickened we dusty creatures into animated praise.

Dear Jesus, you spoke and people were healed, prodigals returned, the hungry were fed, the stingy found abundance, the loveless were embraced, the damned were forgiven.

Gracious God, when we no longer abide in you, we tend to burn things, your creation for starters. We have set your planet on fire this summer. We have lost our way. We have burnt the bodies of our enemies, and our love for each other has withered like grass in July.

You created the heavens not to conquer or weaponize them, but rather to wonder and ponder at the God who made infinity and then became as intimate as our breath.

By your Holy Spirit, when we consider your creation outside of our earth or within our skin, make us to pause . . . to take account of your will and of our own inability to follow it outside of your grace.

Holy God, do not cut us away completely, do not fling us too far from your redemption. Send your Son, the Master Gardener, who can raise the dead.

We pray this as Jesus taught us praying . . .

## ARCHANGELS HEAVING

Gracious God, we have heard your fantastical news of an impending rapture, of trumpet blast, and the archangel heaving out with all its breath.* Do archangels even have breath? Shouting to us that salvation is coming.

God of Genesis, you will lift up the bodies of the dead. Do we even want to see these bodies and how does dust meet the Christ? How does the ancient dead un-crumble to form a form capable of meeting anyone, much less you Jesus in the air?

What is this news you, O Lord, bring to us this morning of rapture and relationship after death?

Holy Spirit, you call this good? We have worries to tend and fears to stoke. There is an invasion coming from Guatemala we are told, soldiers to the border to protect us from the poor.†

And you come to us this morning, dear Jesus, and call us (those left behind), that we are to give our dead and our memory of them, our love of them, our worry of them, to you?

It is enough, dear God, to drive us into the safe arms of reason and rationality.

Jesus, you who are the flesh of God, be sure and include the flesh as you estimate your salvation and plot your rapture. For it is a fleshly death that we fight. It is our breath and more importantly the breath of those we love which need to be recovered.

You, God, holder of the apocalypse, your salvation holds no water unless it holds water and dirt and air and bodies and pandas and rhododendrons and all we touch and are touched by.

Holy Spirit, you will have to breathe on us most heavily, breathe so that we may live as if you and not us hold the future.

Now teach us to pray your prayer . . .

* I Thessalonians 4:13-18
† Central American Migrant Caravans 2018 – Viacrucis del Migrante

## ARTIFICIAL LINES

God of peace, we expressly pray for the Korean summit happening today.*
Move amongst those leaders, so that at least by the end of the day, they have
not made things worse. And if even remotely possible, may they make it
better, better for the Koreans on both sides of the artificial line of hatred.
Better for our children the world over.

Gracious God, thank you for the gift of life. We pray for those who lose it,
who lost it, or who never get a real chance to have it. We pray for those who
take their own life as if it were theirs alone. For aloneness is hell, and out of
its grasp we are called to live.

Dear Jesus, through the power of the Holy Spirit you have come to conquer
death and sin. Forgive us when we see death as the final solution to our
own vulnerability. Our fear is the cause of much killing in your world and
we are sorry.

Dear Jesus, we are especially sorry when we kill in your name, seeking you
to bless our violence. Give us a life worth dying for, but never worth killing
for.

Giver of all that is good, through the power of the Holy Spirit, may our lives
be devoted to your life-giving mission of peace and reconciliation in your
world, so that in our dying we are prepared to be completely reconciled to
you, our creator.

So that in our resurrection, brought by your Spirit, we may see you face to
face.

Through the power of the Holy Spirit, enable us to practice in this kingdom
what you have brought about in the heavenly kingdom, which is the end of
the dominion of death and sin.

We pray this in the name of the one who crossed over lines . . .

* February 2019 between Kim Jong-un and Donald Trump

## BACKSTAGE MOTHER

Holy Merciful God, you art in heaven and your Son strolled upon the earth, taking in the lilies and the halt and blind and skin pocked. For you in Heaven, for your Son's body on earth, we are grateful.

Gracious God, our common life is in tatters and torn asunder. We ask that you sew us back together, like a mother on opening night of the school play, working feverously backstage to patch up a child's costume.

Be our Mother bent over her worktable darning and mending our allegiance to neighbors stitch by tedious painful stitch.

Forgive us our sins, but only in as much as we forgive the sins of our enemies.

We pray for racists, that is white people, interrupt our racism as we dismantle its cancer in our public life.

Finally, we pray for laughter . . . what can we say, it is a deep gift.

In the name of the One who laughs we pray . . .

*BAPTISM* *

Gracious God, this day we pray for Rosemary. Before she was ours she is yours. As we give her back to you, comfort us in our grief and make us to face the future unafraid.

Gracious God, this morning we celebrate the baptism of your Son.

Thank you, Lord, for our own baptisms. Whether we remember them or not, you do. So please hold that memory on our behalf. Whether we were dunked, dipped, sprinkled, immersed, the means was not the end.

The end was your love.

Thank you, Lord, for our baptisms.

Whether we stood by a font held in the arms of someone who loved us or stood in a tank, a trough, a swimming pool, a lake, a river, an ocean, a stream, a pond, or any source of water we could manage to find; we thank you.

The love of your Son is as diverse as the ways we try to draw close to it.

Thank you, Lord, for our baptism. Regardless of how drenched we became when we left our baptismal waters, whether moistened or soaked, you, Holy Spirit, were never quenched. It was never about fulfilling your law; it was always about placing us and those we love closer to your sopping wet grace.

Thank you, Lord, for the church that said the vows over us and promised to hold us to them even as they themselves failed to fully live them out. Thank you for the leaders and pastors who put us under or poured the water over. They were never pure, mostly your endearment for us came through anyway.

We stand before you dank and humid as we pray . . .

* Baptism of the Lord Sunday, Jan 13th 2019

## BEGUILING PEACE

Holy and Merciful God,

May we love boldly by faith in you.

May we live as if peace is more beguiling than war.

May our science be driven by compassion and not survival—for to survive without compassion is intolerable.

May we live as if you have already written the last chapter of our lives and of our world.

May your judgment come with no punishment. May we be removed from comfort until all are comforted. May we know that we are loved as individuals but judged as a people. And the least of these are your people. And boy do you love the least of these—and boy do you get angry when the least of these are not included as our people.

Forgive us our timidity. You gave us the gift of your Son, and we ran real quick and stuffed him some place where he would not get in the way—like when company comes to the house and we sling the loud barky dog in the kennel with a shock collar so our blessed lives will not be intruded upon when the guests arrived.

Let us remember that you are the guest. You are always the guest, and we are merely servants.

As Jesus the guest taught us to pray . . .

## BEMUSED

Holy and Merciful God, we thank thee for this day, for life and love, beauty, and dance.

Gracious God, on this most high holy day of America, where we sacrifice the pig's skin and watch the gladiators battle over a ball in Miami,* we give you thanks for our bodies and the ways we move them, can move them, are blessed to move them.

God of muscles, of fibrils, and amino acids. God who created us to walk, who twitches our proteins and calcium in just the right way so that we will run, hop, skip, or skedaddle. Thank you for delighting in our incredible push against gravity.

We pray for all those whose bodies have worn out, dried up, fossilized, got stuck, or otherwise parted company with their host. May we accept the kind of wisdom that can only come with finitude.

We pray for all those who hate their bodies, who have become enemies with their own selves. We pray for those who starve or cut, who imbibe, ingest, inject beyond boundaries. Pour out your love till we remember to laugh.

We pray for all those who are prevented from dancing, constrained by barbed wire and cages, steel bars and brutality, constrained by the color of skin or the wrong papers. May you give all your children freedom.

And we give you thanks because you choose to cavort and sway and twirl with all, as you gaze at us with a bemused smile, sweaty and poured out . . .

We pray as Jesus, the Lord of the Dance taught us to pray . . .

---

* Super Bowl LIV

## BLACK AND WHITE

Holy and Merciful God, you speak to us this morning from the book of John about light and darkness and how many of us are lovers of darkness and hate the light.

God who trespassed death itself to take away our trespasses, God who created the hues of skin color from dark to light and back again, forgive us for making this about race, and yet race has made us about it.

And so we must ask in the light of black men with dark skin getting shot down by police, in light of how white hates dark we ask that you give us wisdom to know that light and white are not the same.

That white is skin color and comes with racism, but light is spirit and comes with salvation. That there is no salvation where the might of white determines grace.

And one day those of us on top by our whiteness will be thrown down by our hatred of dark until one day, God of white and black, of dark and light, will sweep us up like cinders of sin and uncondemn us, un-judge us, outlove our lovelessness and make us fit for the kingdom of God.

In the name of the one who rode death all the way down and back we pray
. . .

## BLACK

Dear Jesus, thank you for coming into this world and into our lives. Thank you for overcoming all divisions, boundaries, lines, and walls to bring us the Good News that we can be made anew, that in the light of your memory all creation will be redeemed.

Creator God, thank you for all shepherds. Thank you for those managers, protectors, watchers of night, night keepers, those with insomnia, those who work or are wakeful. Those who stay up fretting, worrying, controlling, who deny themselves rest as they look out, wonder, and search; separated from others by delicious sleep.

May we understand that you also hold the night. You hold the darkness. You refused to let light drown out the darkness. That black is a color of your creating and choosing.

Holy Spirit, you do some of your best work at night, in the dark, with black. For without night there is no star, it was in the night that you guided your people to a new land and covenant.

It is in the night that Jesus was asked some of the best questions from Nicodemus.

It was in the night that the Holy Family fled across borders to safety. And it was in the night that the Prince of Peace, the Savior of the world, slipped in.

Sanctifying God, make us at peace with the night. Make us to be at peace with people of all colors. Make us to watch not for danger, but for your messengers. To not build walls against the dark or unknown, but to wait your arrival in the night.

As we wait, let us pray as Jesus taught us praying . . .

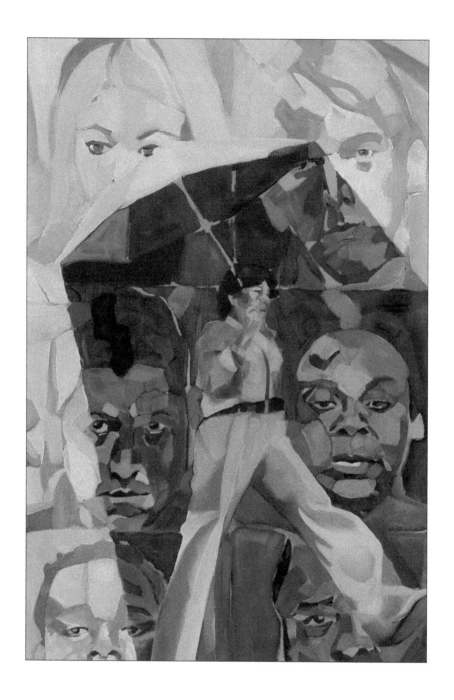

## BODY

Gracious God, thank you for your Body. Thank you, Jesus, for your body—
for being born with a body—coming into this world as embodied word—
for a word that could say yes and say no.

You, Jesus, you cared for your body by allowing others to care for it. You,
Jesus, wanted to touch and be touched. People were wiping their hair on
you and kissing your feet and pouring perfume and oil on you.

You must have been quite smelly and sticky most of your short time on
earth. Did the gnats get stuck in the oil? Did the perfumes mix well together?

Thank you, Jesus, for being the kind of God one could touch.

And you, Jesus, were always touching people. You touched rich and poor
people, ugly people, forlorn people, oozing people, pus-filled people,
petri-dish virused, ringed-wormed, tick-filled, and lice-ridden people you
touched. You were the originator of safe space. Why did you touch so many
people God?

Holy Spirit, could you not have taught us your ideas and justice without
touching us? Perhaps ideas and justice are nothing without a body behind
them.

And then you Jesus, you created a new embodied body, the church.

What does it mean, breathy Spirit, if your body, the church, refuses to
touch? Forgive us when we cross our arms to keep away. And forgive us
when we touch others without compassion and consent. Show us how to
touch without abuse or exploitation. Give us to know when others have
touched us badly and give us the voice to say no.

After all, Crucified Savior, you allowed your body to be killed once and only
one crucifixion was necessary.

We pray as Jesus taught us praying . . .

## BORDERING

Creator God, we lift up to you Norman. Before he was ours he is yours. As we give him back to you, remember us in our loss.

Gracious God, the list of prayer concerns are particularly long this morning. Especially considering the concerns we left off the list. We are especially mindful of families this morning, regardless of where they originated.

You know families across all borders are fragile. Particularly when the borders between countries are a cause of their insecurity.

Precious Spirit, according to Scripture you commanded the Holy Family to flee violence into another country and back again. We are mindful that you are noticeably fond of those who cross borders with nothing but what they carry.

Dear Jesus, we pray for national borders. Whereas we may need them you do not. May we maintain those borders with the reckless compassion by which you lived.

Christ and Lord, you treated borders with disdain and indifference. Including the supreme border of life and death. You transcend all boundaries while loving within them.

Holy Spirit, give us the power to hold the line, in the name of and within the love of Jesus, who held no line accept the one between hospitality and damnation.

Redeemer, make us to know that we will be judged not by how secure we made ourselves, but by how vulnerably we loved the stranger.

You save us not to hoard but to share. How do we share within the complexity of humanity?

In Jesus' name we pray, as he taught us to pray . . .

## BRUISED VISAGE*

Creator God, we lift our adoration to you. You have created the heavens and the earth. You have created all that creeps, crawls, and slithers upon the earth. You have created all that flies and soars over the earth, all that burrows and digs into the earth, and all that walks, skates, slides, and glides on earth's face. You have created all that swims, flaps, and squirts in your oceans.

You have created your kingdom to wiggle, squirm, scoot, skip, or roll.

Almighty God, what does it say about you that you have created so many different ways to move?

What does it say about you that you want life to be in motion . . . and that there is such variety for how creation gets from one place to another?

Holy Spirit, you breathed into all of life and called it good. And then you spiraled it away to be in motion. Dear Holy Spirit, you flicked creation off of your fingers like wet clay on a potter's wheel circling fast, flicked it off off off to move, breathe, and have our being. And we thank you and praise your name.

Dear Jesus, the face of the earth is part of your glory. Forgive us when we bruise that face, or scar it, or tear into it. It was and remains a beautiful face, for earth is a face that reveals your own visage.

How did we ever think it was ours to destroy? Creation is to glorify you. When we kill off a species does it mean your glory is lessoned? What happens to the choir when its members are missing? Forgive us when we act as if we were the creator and not among the created.

Teach us our place by teaching us to pray as Jesus taught . . .

*Gen.1:20-25; Psalm 50:10-12; Job 12:7-10

## BURN BINARIES

Holy Spirit, we come to you, or you come to us, or we meet somewhere in the middle, or however it happens when creatures attempt to encounter their creator without being killed by holiness.

We show up this morning deeply embedded and tied to and in love with our first world, with our first world problems and concerns, our first world fears and the biases based upon them.

Holy Spirit, how did we label worlds into first and thirds, a first world and a third world -just two options for all your people? Just two options?

In the deep of your dovish heart, Holy Spirit, do you divide the world into two halves — a first and a third, a first and last, a world that is first and a world that is third?

Is there within your Holy Spirit a binary division? Life and Death? Crucifixion and Resurrection? Chaos and Creation? Darkness and Light? Truth and Lies? Female and Male? Free and Slave? First and Last? A first world of material power and a third world of poverty and power?

Holy Spirit, within your Trinity, are you two halves or are you three persons laughing or crying as one, in one, for one? Holy Spirit take into your flames and scorch our two until there is one: one Kingdom, one realm, one sphere of power and that power is love and its name is Jesus.

Teach us to pray for this kingdom come as Jesus taught us praying . . .

## CAROUSEL OF CRUELTY

Holy and Merciful God, we thank thee for the gift of your Son and through him for the power of life pushing beyond death.

God of justice beyond our justice, God of justice imposed upon us by the future you are making and have made. What do we do with unjust people? God of fairness, what do we do with unfair people?

God of righteousness, what do we do with unrighteous people . . . especially when we are related to them and must eat stew and watch TV with them in the same room; even though we ourselves are always and only full of kindness and compassion and never never not once even think of them in inhospitable or uncharitable ways?

We pray, Oh God of wonder and revelation, what shall we do with unjust people?

Especially people who we do not know and they who do not know us and yet want to hurt us and we want to hurt them for wanting to hurt us and so we hurt them first and we do not know how long this carousel of cruelty shall circle around your globe as it circles around our hearts.

We pray, O God of joy, how do we believe in the power of rejoicing more than the power of pain real or imagined?

We ask for forgiveness when pain overrides joy. We seek justice when pain overrides joy. We beseech thee, Holy Spirit, to make delighting in you the law of the land.

We pray as Jesus taught us to pray . . .

## CHRISTMAS EVE

God of the Christ Child, we have come this night to say thank you.

In amidst our noise, please hear our gratitude.

Thank you, God, for Mary and Joseph. Thank you for parents everywhere by birth and biology, by choice and adoption. For the good ones and the bad ones. For the ones we can't bear to live without and those we wish we had never met, thank you God, we would not be here without them.

Thank you, God, for Angels. For divine messengers, for those who disturb our peace and cause us fear. For the prophets and winged feathered fools who proclaim that the first shall be last and the last first. And that the powerful shall be thrown down and the downcast raised up.

Thank you, God, for Shepherds. For those who missed out on sleep to care for the vulnerable, the night keepers of the moon and stars, who bear testimony that you love in the dark as intensely as in the light.

God, most of all thank you for Jesus. We couldn't live without him, though you know we have tried.

Jesus the Christ, thank you for coming to love the least, the last, and the lost.

Your message scared us so much we had to kill you.

Holy Spirit, thank you that you are more powerful than our violence. In the resurrection of your Son is our hope.

Holy Spirit, this night as we remember the birth of your Son, may we, by your grace, live in the light of his return, by practicing his life, that is by loving the least, the last, and the lost.

Amen.

## CHRISTMAS EVE II

Gracious God, how did you know we needed a savior? Was it something we did? It sounded like you had Jesus on the tip of your tongue from the beginning; a word spoken with flesh.

How did you know we needed a Jewish Savior, a Savior who is a Palestinian Jew . . . with dark skin and black hair—and perhaps a wide flat nose?

What a mystery, O Creator, that we, with all our hang-ups and phobias, our smells and anger, would find salvation in the Unlike-Other, the one so different from us it almost makes us reach for barbed wire and a cage.

And yet you, Jesus, so much like us it's as if looking at our creator straight in the face when we catch your eye, which we seem to do from time to time.

Jesus, Son of the Most High, you come not to answer our questions, but to act upon our needs. For deep down you saved us not from something but for something. You saved us for putting the last first and the first last; or at least to tell the truth about how firsts and lasts get created.

You, O Jesus Child God, who was born to die, to resurrect and ascend, the first born to live with you again. If we wrote your birth story we would have picked a better way for you to enter into the world than riding upon a donkey embedded in a Virgin's womb.

We would have written in some chariots and a white horse, a tank or two for our God's sake. Yet you were born as you commanded us to live, with enough, with people who loved and cried and suffered and died . . . just like you.

What an odd God you are. Thank you.

You did everything we needed, though little of what we wanted, thank you.

You arrived and all has changed . . . and us along with it and this Christmas we simply wanted to say thank you.

We pray as you taught us praying . . .

## CHRISTMAS EVE III

Hallelujah Christ you are born, a foothold of mercy is established, a beachhead of mysterious grace has appeared.

Hallelujah Christ you are born, witnessed by sheep keepers, a stepfather, assorted farm animals, and a virgin.

Hallelujah Christ you are born, our savior reigns from feeding trough to your right hand.

Hallelujah Christ you are born. And such an odd way for you to arrive. Homeless and undocumented and poor and without choices.

Hallelujah Christ you are born, you should have told us that salvation was so quiet; a baby's whimper, a jackass scratching itself against a door post, a jersey cow chewing cud in the background.

Hallelujah Christ you are born, Satan has just been shown the door, evil has thrown in the towel, the thistles of death are no longer prickly, presidents and kings will bow down, thorns of sin shorn off their tips, the contagion of hatred cured, and all without you killing anyone, not even our enemies.

Hallelujah Christ you are born. Amen!

## CIVIL SERVANTS

Gracious God, we give you Kathy, before she was ours she is yours. As we give Kathy back to you comfort us in our grief.

Jesus, the Son of God, this morning in Scripture we hear of a jailor who arrested Paul for the crime of evangelism. Remember those days, Jesus, when the church told your story so salaciously it got arrested?

God, bless our civil servants. The Jailers, the guards. God, bless the sanitation workers, the court-appointed defenders of the accused and often guilty. The planners, the clerks, the assessors, the admin movers of information.

God, bless our civil servants who plot out the sewage pipes and count off property lines. Who haul away our trash, our refuse, our parts we want to get away from.

Who click on the keyboards and document our lives, our births, our marriage licenses, our deeds, our divorce papers, our permits, our death certificates that make up the bulk of our lives boxed in with our check-marked boxes.

God, bless our civil servants, who offer accreditation and certification, and inspect and ticket and fine or fee or reward our behavior. We like your Son—we are bounded by bodies by the physical small details of life, from boils to burps, we live and move and have our being as physical beings.

Holy Spirit, thank you for the gift of skin. For the skin of others. We pray for the imprisoned and those who imprison. For all those in jail whether the bars be of steel or self-hatred, of our own making or the making of others. We pray for the jailors who are often themselves in a prison of sorts.

Through the liberation of the life, death, and resurrection of Jesus Christ, we pray for freedom.

We pray as Jesus taught us to pray . . .

## CIVIL SERVANT II

Holy and Merciful God, we thank thee for life and love and even for this day.

Lord God, for Roman Centurions, government officials, and bureaucrats everywhere. For those who push the paper, red tape regulations, and follow orders.

For those who zone for growth, and parcel out parcels, and lean in upon their desks, tapping away at computers, pouring over building codes and rules and laws and ledger books.

We thank you.

Lord God, the minor authorities they keep the peace, or at least keep the streets clean and more or less paved. They tamp down on corruption and keep it more or less under the weight of regulations.

And without them God, we would have no hope of getting from A to Z in a rush hour, or of getting balanced scales and uncontaminated food. So we thank you for them.

But Lord God, every once in a while, these bureaucrats, these centurions, these tax collectors, they abuse their power, they follow immoral orders, and they crucify innocent people.

Forgive them, they know what they do, forgive them anyway in the name of the Christ who was crucified by them.

But Holy Spirit, every once in a blue moon you bring a vision and you place it heavily upon these same centurions and tax collectors, these same minor officials, until one day they say something major, "Truly this was the Son of God!" or "Send for Peter in Joppa for in Jesus all means all!"

And we are left to wonder, who are you, God of Jews and Gentiles, that you would bestow such visions upon such ordinary, underappreciated, and corruptible people, like ourselves?

As we wonder we pray, as Jesus taught us to pray . . .

## CONFIRMATION

Holy and Merciful God, we thank you for your Holy Spirit bouncing embers off our dullard heads, waking us up to where you are leading and prodding and sometimes, rather impatiently we must say, moving us to be peacemakers and reconcilers and forgivers and all the other ways Christians are to announce the inauguration of your dominion.

For, quite frankly, if we may be direct with your Holiness, we have enough Christians who, however regretfully, believe in war and believe in armies and believe in Smith & Wesson and understand violence to be necessary and therefore a good thing and should therefore be inflicted by good Christians.

Forgive us for doing things you never would; and forgive us when we do it in your name, seeking your endorsement.

Holy Spirit, like a dove of peace flying with such fragility, alight upon our confirmands this day. It will be difficult to follow you throughout their lives. They do not stand a chance of loving you and loving neighbor, without you and without us, and we them.

The same goes for those graduating this spring.

Keep them close to the church. But not just any kind of church. Keep them close to the kind of church that will tell them the truth, that they are mortal and one day will die, and that before that happens they will leave a lot of good things left undone, and they will hurt others whether they mean to or not, and that you already know all this ahead of time, and that you are really good at bringing all prodigals home, and when you do, there is an awful lot of joy.

To the one who constantly searches for wayward strangers we pray . . .

## CORNERS OF HEART

Holy and Merciful God, we thank thee for life, your love, and the gift of your Son to all the world.

We pray for your child Clare. Before he was ours, he is yours. Comfort us in our grief as we wait in the sure and certain hope of his resurrection from the dead in love.

Creator God, our world is in travail, and there does not seem to be one corner without it. You know this, and we need to tell you anyway. If not for your sake then at least for ours.

Have mercy on us. Have mercy on this world.

We pray for the corners of the world that we consider helpless, the Haiti's and Bangladesh's, the North Korea's, and the Sierra Leone's.

We pray for our helplessness, may it not turn into fear, for we do nasty things when we are frightened.

We pray for our bodies and souls and those of our enemies. Through the power of your Spirit please give us the power to heal, or at least give us the wisdom to not make things worse.

We pray for the church. We do our best work when tenderness is needed.

May we feel your presence like a cold compress on a fevered brow.

For it is by your presence that we become generous in a time of hoarding.

Mostly Dear Jesus, we thank you. Thank you for your ever-living compassion to all corners of your world and all corners of our hearts.

We pray as Jesus taught us to pray . . .

## CRAMMED FULL OF LOSERS

Holy and Merciful God, we thank thee for life and love and laboratory researchers.

We thank you for nursing home managers and respiratory therapists. Thank you for truck drivers and we can't believe we are thanking you for postal workers but there it is God, in this time in our world, thank you for people who deliver mail.

We thank you for governors who understand science, and scientists who understand that humans are mortal.

Gracious God, we do like our war. We go to war with anybody. Now we are at war with a virus. Dear Jesus, there are frontlines and a Homefront and soldiers who are really hospital receptionists or grocery store clerks but whom we call soldiers because we value soldiers but not hospital receptionists or grocery store clerks.

O Prince of Peace, stop our wars. Stop us from trying to win something for once. For there will be winners and losers in a fight. We may win the economy but not the lives of our elderly. We may win the lives of our elderly but not our jobs.

We pray for the hope in our helplessness. For by our helplessness we will turn to you. You, O Holy one who triumphed by losing. By your Holy Spirit who taught us to lose our lives for the sake of your kingdom.

God who created us and this twirling globe crammed full of winners and losers, we pray as Jesus taught us to pray . . .

## CRUST

Gracious God, thank you for the beauty of this earth. Thank you for creating an earth which can sustain impact, for we humans walk heavy across its crust.

You must be an awesome God, so full of wonder to give such gifts like giraffes and children and old people and also platypus ducks. We do not know what you were thinking Lord. May our lack of knowledge give us pause.

Forgiving God, forgive us when we choose correctness over kindness. Give us some humility with our right causes. Give us a love for those we bitterly are at odds with. May we speak our truth without assuming it is The Truth.

Holy Spirit, give us the power to forgive our enemies and the desire to do so.

Creator Christ, thank for the joy of work. Jesus the Carpenter, thank you for giving us jobs and the purpose and satisfaction that goes with completing them. Forgive us when we seek to exploit instead of to ponder; to use instead of to pray.

By the power of your Spirit, sustain us for the undramatic, tedious, the unheralded, and boring-never-ending work of loving you, loving our neighbors, and loving your creation.

We pray as Jesus taught us . . .

## DO YOU LOVE ME?*

O Jesus who gathers your betrayers together to go fishing and have breakfast, whoever thought that having fish and baguettes with cowards was the way to start a church?

But then, as we look around at ourselves, why would we think any different?

You come back from the dead to catch carp or steelhead or whatever it is that comes out of Lake Tiberias, and you make a charcoal fire, and while the fish is sizzling and popping and the bread is being sliced, you ask of Simon Peter and Thomas and Nathanael and us, you ask, "Do you love me?"

Do we love you, Jesus? What kind of question is that? Do you love me is a question of longing and uncertainty. Do you love me is what one lover asks for assurance, for foundation, for a starting point.

It's what one asks when you need somewhere to land, it's a question of possibility, it is a bridgehead, it is an outcropping over an abyss, it is to haul one's self up to a precipice and yell, "Catch me I'm falling into you."

We adore you, O Christ, because after what you know about us you still fling your body to us. And what we know about you we want to catch it.

Do you love me?

To the one who comes to us as a question we pray . . .

* John 21:15

## EASTER

Gracious God, Giver of new life, Author of birth, Defeater of death, the Power of love, what a wonder you make this day.

Resurrected Christ, server of the poor, servant of the broken, listener of those who lost and failed and died and sinned. You are the pioneer of our faith – the first through the breach of death, catapulting into life after death, and like a sling shot to a rock you snatch us along with you.

Though we may forget you 7 times 70 over, your strength and your will to love will infinitely match our willful amnesia.

Holy Spirit, Advocate of life, fierce Protector of the vulnerable, tender Mother to the addicted and the mentally ill, Holy Spirit you are the insistent nagging Bringer of restlessness. You announce that the Kingdom has come . . . and it includes our enemies.

This day we come, however quietly, however hesitantly, however grudgingly . . .

This day we come, however joyfully, however humorlessly, however mockingly . . .

This day we come, and our coming is our yes. It is our response. Today at this moment, it is the truest we can say thank you for giving the created order hope.

Death has lost its sting, memory is restored, and we are not alone.

It is Easter Morning and Jesus is risen from the dead. Hallelujah.

## EATING LAMBS*

Holy and Merciful God, we thank thee for life and love and the expected return of your Son.

Creator God, what does it mean that you delight in us? That our very existence as your creation gives you joy?

We have a strong suspicion that such joy is more about who you are as God than who we are as your people.

Gracious God, you proclaim your word this morning through the prophet Isaiah. This morning the prophet Isaiah coos and sooths and whispers and wails and booms and boasts that there is a new creation coming.

Crucified Christ, you claim that one day the lion will eat straw like the ox and that the wolf and the lamb shall feed together. O Lord, when you said feeding together, did you mean that the wolf will be feeding *upon* the lamb or *beside* the lamb?

We have to ask, dear Jesus, in light of what we have seen and what we see. In the dark light of gas chambers and ovens built for the shape of humans, in flag draped walls, and xenophobia, may your good news be as powerful as unquestioned patriotism and militarized nationalism.

Holy Spirit, you claim that in the days to come a generation will be born for peace, and no more shall infants be born but for a day, and no more shall people be without homes, and no more shall the sound of weeping be heard.

By your power may those days to come impel us to fearless gratitude today. By your power may the days to come uproot cynicism and make way for relationship. Until we see in the stranger the same kind of joy you see in us.

We pray as Jesus taught his fearless followers to pray . . .

* Isaiah 65: 17-25

## EVERY JOT AND TITTLE

Holy and Merciful God, we thank thee for thy flaming Spirit, your Son's breath, and even for this day.

Gracious God, it is Pentecost, it is the day we celebrate the giving of your flaming Spirit to the world through your church.

The church, a bunch of forgiving, loving, fallible, sinning, messy, group of vipers and saints all mixed-up-as-one, that the world has ever seen.

We thank thee all powerful God for your flitter(y) and fiery Spirit blazing up upon and all over your followers like syrup on hot pancakes.

Now the church has a mission, now the Christian community has a purpose, now your people have a mandate.

The Holy Spirit has come, Jesus's promise is fulfilled, and we have a command to follow.

Now by your powerful Spirit we get to tell every stick, jot, and tittle, every toad tree, and sunset, every person of every hue, creed, and orientation the Good News that a savior is born, that

The Injustice of disease . . . will be healed,

That the murder of black men . . . will be murdered

That Racism as a power of death . . . will die

That Death itself . . . will be flung into a lake of fire.

That there is healing for our nation, that enemies will be reconciled, that guns will be smashed into irrelevance, that the dirt and the water and the air will find sabbath, and that we can practice all this today by the power of this same Spirit,

In the name of the one who came to kick start resurrection we pray . . .

## FAIRLY WELL ADJUSTED

Holy and Merciful God, we thank thee for life and love and even for this day.

We thank you for Sundays, where we come together to remember that you found us first, not of our own doing, but out of your desire. You, unafraid, found where we were hiding and you placed your cross upon us and said, "Tag you're it."

Dear God, forgive us our newsfeeds. We often forget that what we consider news is not newsworthy. May our fears and fantasies be captured by the Good News of your Son who loves us to death and back.

We pray for the broken hearted, for whom life has become a burden. We do not know what to do with those who do not particularly want anything done to them. May you, and by you we mean ourselves, be a companion to them as they walk the long loneliness.

We pray for people who are hungry. Most of the time we do not know what to do about people who do not eat as you created them to eat. Or we know but do not do it, as we slide our next meal into our throats. Give us the courage, through the power of your Holy Spirit, to feed hungry people like we ourselves would want to be fed.

We pray for those who are fairly well adjusted and have adapted quite nicely to this world as it is. Prick us from our alliances with loveless power. Especially that power which corrupts the dirt, the air, the water.

You, O Lord, have never given up on us or on this earth. You delight in us, even before we know what delight means.

As those who have been wooed by delight we pray as Jesus taught us to pray, . . .

## FAITH

Holy and Merciful God, we thank you for the gift of life, your Son our Savior, and even for this day.

Well God, we give to you our faith, which is really a gift from you anyway, as we could not have faith without you giving us the power to have faith and without giving us your Son to have faith in, so in as much as it could be ours we offer it back to you, do with it what you will.

Dear Christ, we do not quite understand how all of this is supposed to work when it comes to faith, how much is yours and how much is ours. What is your responsibility and what is ours?

At some point we sound like kids in the back seat of a long ride arguing over the invisible line, allegedly separating in equal parts whose side is whose, all the while demanding fairness.

Which side belongs to you, O Lord, and which side belongs to us? Do you do virus and we do war? Did you do cancer and we do racism? Did you give us the apple and we ate it? Who was responsible for what?

We do not know if you can see our faith, it often seems invisible to us much of the time. Maybe because we are always arguing about what is fair and staking out our claim like children fighting over the morning box of cereal.

But it's the best we can muster today. For we are lonely and a bit tired and a bit more afraid and if we must be honest not very good at sharing.

And it is only because your Son, our Lord was able to muster everything and share everything and it is this everything that we dive into like a sleeping bag at a damp fireless camp site in the dark.

We humbly beg you to be our Holy Spirit of fire, lighting our kindness out into the night.

In the name of the One who never fears and always shares we pray . . .

## FEAR

Holy and Merciful God, we thank thee for life, your love, and a Son more powerful than what ails us.

We thank you for Elwyn. Before he was ours he is yours. Comfort us in our grief as we await with assurance the time where we all may feast with one another without anyone going hungry.

O Deep Dear Beloved God of us all, we abide in you, and you abide in us, and we all abide together, and yet we seem not to like each other very much. How do we love one another if we do not like each other?

Abiding Awaiting Holy Spirit, do you even like us? Do you have to like us in order to save us? And do we have to love you in order to confess that Jesus is the Son of God?

And in all this loving and abiding and liking and saving, when is dinner? Will dinner be served to hungry people while we abide and like and love?

We are told that perfect love casts out fear, our love must be far from perfect, because we have a lot of fear. We have fear in our stomachs, and fear with our money, and fear in our politics, and fear in hospitals, and in funeral homes, and fear of our neighbors. Fear of the police, fear of poor people who come north, fear of black people who move in next door, fear of white people in charge.

We have fear in all kinds of things. If you give us something, God, believe me we will come to fear it.

You give us a Son, we will fear him to death. But he will fear death to hell and come back in love.

To the one who sweeps aside our fears we pray . . .

## FIRST TOUCH*

All Merciful and Mighty God, we thank you even for this day.

For today, Dear Jesus, you teach us to be disciples by washing our feet. You stoop down low the day before you will be lifted up high on a cross. Before your crucifixion, you wash our feet.

What an odd way to teach discipleship.

What does it mean, dear Christ, that the first time you ever touch us, you touch us on our feet? Perhaps we would have picked a different body part, what with feet being so . . . hidden.

You called us, O Christ, you pulled us away from our lives and loves to follow you. You taught us, you commanded us and chastised us, you sent us out in your name. We have eaten with you, argued with you, we have witnessed your miracles and how you touched others, but until now, after all the time we have spent with you, this is the first time you ever-ever took your brown calloused carpenter hands and held our flesh.

The day before your flesh will be torn apart.

Thank you for your touch. Forgive us when we exchange beliefs for small, quiet, odd, vulnerable, fleshy touch.

* John 13

## FOR THE FARMERS

Holy and Merciful God, we thank thee for this day and all life.

We pray for farmers everywhere. Whether they use a $100,000 tractor or a wooden hoe. We pray for those who grow our food and are rarely considered by those who eat it.

We pray for farmers who pray for good weather. For those who constantly listen to forecasts and fret over hail and too much rain, or not enough rain, or rain that comes at the wrong time, who have to hurry to beat the rain, or have to wait because of the rain, who are at the mercy of rain and sun and wind and temperature and soil and markets.

We pray for farmers.

Jesus, in your Scripture you often tell us of sowers and reapers. Your disciples break bread and eat dinners, they walk through fields of grain taking their fill. We do not know O Lord, what the grain farmers thought about your disciples who are walking in their fields, taking grain, and breaking stalks.

Jesus, you ask us to be planted in your soil, to hold fast to honesty, to have a good heart, to bear your fruit, to be patient, and to endure. It sounds like hard work. Through the power of your Holy Spirit, transform our belief in our own ability and goodness into a simple reliance upon you.

We pray as Jesus taught us to pray . . .

## FORTY FIFTH

Holy and Merciful God, we thank thee for thy Son whose coming and presence we celebrate this season. In him there is no darkness at all, not even north of the 45$^{th}$ parallel.

Well Lord we impeached a president this week.* Are you proud of us? Did we do your will . . . or our own? Or is it always a mix? Did we body check a bully, or did we give license to our biases? Or did we do both? Is it always a both with you?

God of eternal covenant, we place before you our actions, may they be worthy of the life, death, and resurrection of your Son.

God of new life, we pray for families everywhere, who like your Holy Family are forced to move, to leave in the name of bureaucracy and tax roles and national security. We pray for migrants and the undocumented, for those who are held hostage by borders. For those lying in cages in Houston or mangers in Bethlehem.

May our lust for safety be broken by your Spirit more powerful than what we can imagine.

We pray as Jesus taught us to pray . . .

* 1$^{st}$ Impeachment of Donald Trump December 18, 2019

## FRETTING

Gracious God, thank you for your love. Thank you for the gift of life. We are especially mindful of the gift of life you have given Alice. You, Creator God, claimed Alice as your own. You claim her now in your love without end, more powerful than death.

Sustaining Holy Spirit, we pray for rest. We pray for Sabbath. Refresh us by your word. Fling away from us a life of fretting, of nagging fretting. You do not have time for the fretters, Lord. You have no time to fret. Turn our fretting into pondering. Turn our anxiety into awe. Turn our worries into wonder.

Creator God, give us a home, give us this day daily bread, and clean water, and heat, and dignity, and safety, and love, and for our enemies. And for those of us who have an abundance of these, give us generosity, especially of our time.

Dear Jesus, work within us till we see our neighbors in ourselves. Jesus, please make us to treat others as we ourselves would want to be treated. But most of all, give us the intelligence to rest today. To slow down. To seek the still dark places. To pay attention without judgment to where you might be.

We pray as Jesus taught us praying . . .

## FRIENDSHIP*

Holy and Merciful God, we thank thee for your Son Christ Jesus, for the Holy Spirit, and thank you for mothers, without whom we would not be.

Abiding God, who appoints us, and choses us, and selects us, and rolls away the stones from under which we have crawled, carrying us into the sunlight, blowing off the roly-polies and asking, "Do you want to be friends?"

We didn't know friendship was possible with the King of Glory. We knew we could believe in you, Jesus, and have faith in you and be kind in your name and crucify systems of hatred upon you till they ground down into fine nothing . . . but friendship?

We didn't know friendship was possible with you, O Lord of Lords.

Are you the kind of friend who tells us the truth about love?

That when you say you love us, you mean you love those we hate. You hold the love we cannot or will not hold on our behalf, until one day we will hold it for ourselves.

For those anywhere who are ground down by loveless men with guns, we pray for their witness. We pray until victims are turned into agents. We pray until our friendship with you includes our friendship with those ground down by loveless men with guns.

We pray until the guns of loveless men are ground down into fine nothing.

To our loving Friend we pray . . .

* John 15

## GUESTS NOT HOST

Holy and Merciful God, this Epiphany we are thankful to you as the teller of secrets, Holy and Epiphanous Lord, you are the revealer of all mysteries, except the mysteries we get interested in like; Is Big Foot real? What's in Area 51? Why do children suffer? What happens when we die?

Except the mystery of how to tell the difference in your voice when you order Abraham to kill Isaac, and your voice when you say spare his life. How are we to tell the difference in your voice? It seems an important mystery to untangle. Is there a tremble in it, does it quiver a bit with one commandment and become more steady with the other?

O Great Revealer of mystery, the Holder of life and death, there is really only one secret you have revealed to us which is, according to your Scripture, the mystery of whether we get into your family.

By your Spirit with the biggest spoiler alert of them all, you reveal to us that YES, through Christ we are adopted!

Covenantal God, given what happens to your family—the slavery, the exile, the holocaust . . . perhaps becoming a family member isn't all it's cracked up to be.

And yet heir to the promise of Christ, the relationship of life, is where we find home.

And that everything we do, we do as guests. All our ethics, all our desires, all the rules we want everyone to obey, we only always do them as invited guests, and never the host.

So by the power of your Holy Spirit, give us the politeness of guests, the willingness to set up extra chairs at the dinner table, to step aside and let others get served first, to ask if there is anything we can do to help . . .

In the name of the one who gave us access to God we pray . . .

## GUN STORES OF EGYPT*

God of Compassion, you tell us that you listen to the cries of the orphans and the widows. After last week in Las Vegas there are now more orphans and widows in the world . . . are you listening?†

How do we practice our faith in the midst of murder and suicide? How is your Son raised as Lord as people fall to the ground?

And God of Repentance, how have we strayed from your path of peace? After all, you did not pull the trigger, or sell the gun, or enshrine the right to own it . . . that was our doing.

Forgiving-Seeking-God, as your prophet Isaiah rebukes, do we look for safety in the gun stores of Egypt . . . outside of your protection?

God of Forgiveness, bring us back home to trust in your quiet and return to your rest.

God of Endings, through your Holy Spirit you are bringing a new "Kingdom come on earth as it already is in heaven;" a kingdom of peace. And we pray for it now . . . for what else can we do?

* Isaiah 30

† This prayer was offered after the mass shooting in Las Vegas October 1, 2017

## HAGAR'S LAMENTATION

All Powerful and Merciful God we come before you this morning.

We who sit in darkness thought we saw a light on the horizon, perhaps it was only gun muzzle flashes in New Zealand.* We who sit amongst your silence thought we heard a voice crying out in the wilderness, perhaps it was only Hagar's lamentation over Ishmael's children.

Christ Crucified, this morning we mourn for our Muslim brothers and sisters, your children, killed for their religion. We are sorry for their deaths. We are sorry for all the deaths of all your children who died because they worshipped.

As we hear the sounds of spring time and new life, we are ever mindful of how tenuous breathing can be.

All we can do is breathe your Holy Spirit into our muscle fibers and bone flakes until we exhale our fear speaking out loud against evil. Our hope, Holy Spirit, is not in our power to tinker but in your power to transform. Turn all crucifixion towards Easter, shape us to be those who practice resurrection.

We pray as Jesus taught us praying . . .

* Shooting in New Zealand, March 15, 2019

## HATE

Holy and Merciful God, we thank thee for your tender mercies, your open adoption, and even for this day.

It is so odd of you God to add to your family, to increase your household, to go through not simply death but also the horrors of living so that more of us could be adopted as your kin.

It is not so clear, God whose-love-beats-back-death's-dominion, it is not so clear how to live in a time of hate. Perhaps a time of hate is all the time there is. Perhaps, O Lord of Cain and Able, of Sarah and Hagar, there has never been a time where we do not hate.

O Lord of Jacob and Esau, hate is so pervasive we have to pass a law to criminalize it. Hate is a crime now; hate crimes. But can we really outlaw hate? Can we really cause hate to end by making it illegal?

What, O Lord of newness, what makes a mass shooting a mass? Is it a mass like a cancer can be a mass? Would one person murdered constitute a mass shooting for those who loved the one?

How come, O Holy Spirit, you spent so much time sewing Jew and Gentile together, if we keep ripping out the seams?

O Jesus, whose death came at the hands of hatred, this is what we know:

In your tortured body you bring hater and hated together, this is how you create a family and you dare us to do the same . . . this is where you are going . . . we can come along or not.

To the one who adopts us, without a care we pray . . .

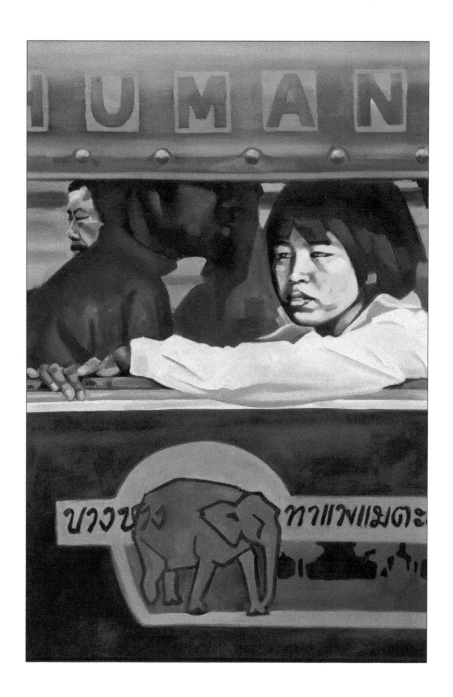

## HATE LIKE GOD

Gracious and Holy God, you are the Creator of heaven and earth, the skies, the burrows, fields and furrows, and into the deepest deep.

Your Son holds the keys of heaven and hell. We would sure appreciate it if you would open the doors of heaven wider for those we love and agree with, while keeping the gates of hell closed-up-tight.

Unless it concerns our enemies dear Jesus, and then we would like you to send them straight into the flames, the eternal ones too, not the flames that get blown out by your Spirit's reconciling wind.

O Lord, especially fling into the pit those who voted against us in the last election, God do we hate them . . . but you do not. You gave them life and died their death. Is it true God that the only thing you hate is when we hate in your name? For our enemies are your friends.

Dear Jesus, who touched the outcast, especially the working class. Dear Jesus, who touched the outcast, especially the rich, whom everyone envies but few help into the Kingdom. We pray for the power to love.

O Holy Spirit, forgive us our deadly righteousness. Take away our isolation. Birth us to seek out the "other" whomever the "other" might be for us.

Make us to sow peace where there is hatred, starting but never ending within our own hearts. Amen.

## IMAGE OF ENEMIES

Holy and Merciful God, we thank thee for your Son our liberation, your Spirit our life, and even for this day.

We give thanks for Bill, a child of your own redeeming, a member of your covenant, a participant in your people. Receive him into your salvation, which is to abide in you. Comfort us in our grief as we lay down the love and responsibility of walking with him through his life. Our watch is done, our worries are over, in Christ all is at peace.

Gracious God, you may have formed us in your image, but either your image is horribly different than we imagined or somehow we forgot that when we looked into the faces of our opponents we were staring into a mirror of you.

God of Promise, you pledged to be our God. We did not expect you to pledge the same to our opponents. For we believe that only one side is blessed by you and thus the other side must be cursed by you.

And that we are on the side of good and that our opponents are on the side of evil. And that our opinions, and not your pledge, determine who is good and who is evil.

God, your love of our opponents is disheartening. You and only you determine good and evil. Only you can birth and only you can take retribution. Forgive us when we attempt to take away what is yours, for vengeance belongs only and always to you.

In Jesus, the one whose vengeance looked like an empty tomb we pray . . .

## INOCULATED BODIES

Holy and Merciful God, we thank thee for your love, research laboratories, and even for this day. You, O Lord of darkness and of light, to you goes salvation. Teach us the truth that whatever we seek from the hands of medicine, it will not keep us from death, merely hold it off for a while, at least for those who can afford it.

Father and Mother to this earth, you are our Alpha and Omega, our beginning and our end, and one day you will hold our inoculated dead bodies that we tried so hard to keep safe, and you will raise us in resurrection to glorify you. By your Spirit, may we give our allegiance to that which is eternal.

We pray for those who have lost their jobs and those who have lost their businesses. Comfort them in their grief. We, by your Spirit, must be responsible to them. You, God's Son, seated at the right hand of the Father, may not need money in heaven, but it comes in handy down here.

And yet, O Lord, forgive us when our elderly become a burden. Tell us, God of Life, how many old people should die so we can get a fresh hamburger?* We have truly traded existence for love . . . all we can say is sorry.

We pray for those who were already living in an uncertain time before the middle and upper classes discovered it through COVID. We pray for the poor, the homeless, those without advocates, bring them to the front of the line.

We pray for those who are bereft of friendship. Who are bereft of kisses and caresses, who sit and wait and wait some more, it is rare that we can help our neighbors, by simply waiting. So by your Spirit give us patience to wait our turn.

Amen.

---

* COVID Pandemic – pushing to open from quarantine

## KEEPING GOMER

Gracious God, you are the Creator of heaven and earth. You are the Originator of life, and you give us the monsters of the deep, the heavens, the blood moon, and the bright orb of Mars.

You are the giver of rain and sun—our Creator, Sustainer, Judge, and Redeemer. By your Spirit you formed a people forged in covenant, lost in slavery, and freed for witness.

Gracious God, you formed us, a people, who loved you and betrayed you and came back to you only to leave again. A people, O Lord, who you had to go through hell's teeth to drag back over and over and over like a mother with an angry toddler fed up with 'awake time' seeking a nap.

Holy Spirit, you brought forth the church and brought us into its communion. We hate it, we love it, we cannot live without it, though we wonder at least once a week if leaving it would be a decent idea.

Dear Jesus, you blew your breath across our faces until we noticed, however briefly, our condition and your invitation to live without violence. You taught us to forgive enemies, feed hungry people, and to seek out the least, the last, and the lost with the Good News that in your house the last will be first and the first will be last.

Dear Jesus, though you may have cast some of us to the back of the line, we are grateful that we still get to remain in line, for your glory is bright even in the rear.

Thank you for putting up with us, for allowing us to forgive you, for revealing enough of you to sustain us for another day, a day of your creation.

And now Jesus, lead us to pray as you first led us praying . . .

## LAWFULLY LIVED LIVES

Holy and Merciful God, your Son our Savior was crucified to keep the law and to keep the peace.

Your Son was killed to fulfill the law of the land and to keep order in the city; to pacify the crowds.

How do you wish us to proceed when our leaders today call for law and order?

Jesus, you overturned tables and upset money makers and created chaos. You made clean what we made unclean, you touched the wicked, and forgave murderers. You canceled out sin, you called your followers into danger, you even reversed the nature of death itself, and generally caused havoc to the way we ordered ourselves.

Why . . . it is like everywhere you went you sowed discord and got somebody angry. Although, come to think of it, no one you healed no matter how important, no one you healed no matter how unimportant, no one you healed ever got angry with you.

What is it God? What is the reason that telling the world a new kingdom was at hand really, and I mean really, got a lot of important people angry?

And you call us to do the same in your name. And the only way we will lift our heads from our ordered and lawfully lived lives is if you love us so much we have no other choice but to love our neighbors in the same disorderly way.

What does it mean that your disciples were so in love with you they caused riots and got arrested and generally did not get along well with the authorities?

So in the name of the one who destabilized order and became a new law unto himself we pray . . .

## LESS JEWISH

Gracious God, send us another savior. Make him better than the one before. Make him to bless our violence, not curse it.

Make him to like us more and to condemn us less, more Christian, and less Jewish, if you don't mind.

Holy God, send us another son. We promise to pay attention this time.

One who will control our enemies, better yet send us an idol, not a prophet. Send us a graven image of ourselves, so that we may take selfies forever, beyond the grave.

God of new birth, send us a son who, if he can't give us eternal life of love, will at least give us a never-ending one. If he cannot raise us from the dead, at least take away death, or at least reserve death only for our enemies.

Redeemer God, give us a human, not a God. Give us someone who can inspire us to work harder, that we may save ourselves in the way we believe we must be saved.

Creator God, can you take Jesus back? He was too demanding anyway, too unwavering with his insistence that suffering is not the worst, but rather separation is – which is purity without compassion – relationship without forgiveness – touch without tenderness.

Send us a politician we can control . . . oh no! Never mind, we have enough politicians.

NO GOD! Ignore us. We do not know for what we ask. You give us Jesus, a Jew, from Palestine, dark scarred skin, the Son of the Living God. The One who holds the keys to heaven and hell. And the One who is on his knees washing the feet of his betrayers. We like clean feet. This Savior is enough. Thank you for Jesus.

This Jesus who taught us to pray . . .

## LESSER SAINTS

Holy and Merciful God, we thank you for remembering us. Your memory creates us. We are not people until you call us to be a people.

May our memory of your covenant command our ethics—which is just another way of saying our allegiances and the passions and perversions we really care about.

May our allegiance to your Son, who commanded us not to safety but to peace; may our allegiance to your Son be the pair of glasses we put on to see our neighbor, even the neighbors who are just plain nasty and have little regard for our goals, dream boards, personal mission statements, and bald face ambitions.

May our memory of your covenant cause us to love the folks who do not love us back.

Someone must love these nasty unlovable neighbors, and you have picked us. And we do not like it one bit, God. So, we must hide behind your cross and listen to your sermons and bask in the light of your resurrection and huddle with the other followers you have also called, which is the church, and ask for your Holy Spirit to make us into saints.

But if we may ask so humbly, make us into one of the Saints who have no feast day and for whom nobody will remember later. Make us into one of those kinds of saints.

But not like the kind who get killed for their love of you. Please let us avoid the feast-day saints, O Lord.

May our faith in you be stronger than our loneliness and aloneness. May the faith you have in us, which is the same thing as your faith that makes us alive in the first place—may that faith propel us to be bold.

In boldness your Son taught us to pray . . .

## LUSTROUS TALONS*

Light-flinging God, Light-Shining Jesus, Light-breathing Spirit – O praise to you—The in-breaking, the light breaking, the blinding boom and awe of you, Jesus Christ, recognized by no one; except angels, shepherds, a handful of astrologers, while a bovine or two indifferently chews cud in the background.

Terrifying Lighting Epiphanous God, O praise to you. In your word you burned in bushes and bones, you kindled in a baking pillar of fire by night guiding your people across a glimmering desert.

You in the end fanatically flung death out into an apocryphal lake of fire causing death to die, and you broke out most irresponsibly and prophetically for all the world to see in your Jewish Son Jesus.

What gifts do you bring to us, and not just us, but also our enemies and your earth that we both live upon as well?

Scintillating Spirit—O Praise to you—embers of glory bouncing off your lustrous talons as you pin the stars to your cosmic corkboard, your beauty and justice arc over this glittering earth, what do you compel us to do, what do we know we need to do but are a bit afraid of doing it? What of your image do you grace us to reflect?

O Son of humanity – O Praise to you – you are an arsonist to death and sin. Your deafening gurgles of joy emanating from a flammable manger – your fire of fondness for us is a source of gratitude without end.

We are grateful that we amuse you . . . so much . . . O Three Person God.

Out of our gratitude we pray, as Jesus taught us to pray . . .

* Epiphany Sunday

## MEMORIAL DAY

Gracious God, this is Memorial Day weekend. It is a weekend where we lift up the dead to your care and memory. And so we hold before you our dead, both the brave and the cowards, those who stood steady and those who did not. Most of them are gone from our memory but never from yours.

We lift up to you, Gracious Holy Spirit, those who served in tradition and those who served outside accepted tradition. Both served out of the best conscience they could muster.

We pray for the kind, the upstanding, the resilient, and also the stingy, the cruel, and those who caved.

Holy Jesus, Lover of our enemies, we bring before your care and memory both those on our side and those on the other side, hoping that in the Kingdom of God there will be no more sides.

Creating God, we make sides because you have made us to be a species that needs categories, and threat assessments, and safety. May we strive for safety without violence, labeling without lethality, and categorizing without colonization.

You love us and you love those we hate. May our bafflement at your uncompromising Grace give us pause . . . before we cause more death in our name, or in yours, for it is in Your Name O Jesus that we pray . . .

## MOB

God of a Crucified Christ, you know what it is like to be murdered by mob violence.

We pray for the mob who assaulted the U.S. Capital on Wednesday and for the President who told them to do it.* How did we as a country get so lost? Without going in a different direction, we will not be found. Give us the power to repent.

Jesus our Agitator and Transformer, our Jewish Prophet, you O Jesus, you overturned the tables of money without killing the money changers.

You warned of an impending judgment, you did not bash a policeman's head with a fire extinguisher. If we cause death and mayhem let us at least be clear, we do it in the name of America and not yours.

You O Jesus, instigator of prophetic imagination, there was enough misplaced allegiance last Wednesday to almost forget our baptism and how you saved creation without any help from us.

There was enough destruction last Wednesday to almost forget that you are Lord, that you reign supreme over all racial supremacists, and that we as your body are to love our enemies.

You, O Lover, more powerful than nations, make us to remember the world was not transformed on a Wednesday but on a Friday. And that you gave your response to mob violence not with more violence but with resurrection three days later.

By the power of the Holy Spirit, harness our anger and turn it into lamentation. For there is much to lament. Give us the power to cry.

In the name of the one who overturned lives and loves and cried over the dead we pray . . .

* Capital Insurrection Jan 6, 2021

## MOTHER'S DAY

Holy and Merciful God, we thank thee for all things, even for this day.

Mothering God, thank you for mothers, the bad ones and the good ones, but especially the good ones. Regardless, without either . . . we would not be.

Mothering God, thank you for mothers who use their bodies to feed their babies, to shelter their toddlers, to push and pull them away from childhood into adulthood, who grind out day after day, and who joyously receive moment after moment, the love of their kids in all its complexity and ambiguity; whole-hearted and full-throated, mucus-coated, peanut-smeared love.

We are especially vigilant and watchful, Adventist Christ, for your coming Kingdom. A Kingdom where no mothers will ever have to experience the loss of their children for any reason.

Mothering God, we are especially mindful of those mothers who have lost their children most recently to violence and face their first Mother's Day without them. Comfort them as you attempted to comfort Rachel weeping for her lost children.

Mothering God, grant us the gifts of nurture and compassion for our children, and for the children who were birthed elsewhere by other mothers. May our love for their kids transcend love of our country.

Mothering God, grant us the desire and power to care for your earth, our great incubator of life without which nothing would survive. Convert us from being consumers to being stewards.

We pray as Jesus taught us to pray . . .

## MOUSY HEARTS*

O Jesus who whips up and castigates and drives off the livestock—and our livelihoods with them.

Is zeal the same thing as a temper tantrum? What makes one zealous for the Lord? What, O Jesus, made you zealous for your Father's house?

When we think of cleansing a temple, we think of floor wax and painting the trim along the southside windows. When you think of cleansing a temple, you mean an exorcism. A purging of the powers of death. You mean tearing asunder our mousy faintheartedness.

You mean killing death, and we mean keeping safe.

You collapse systems by which we make meaning and money.

O Jewish Jesus, you have God to worship, we have a religion to tend to.

And so, as you thundered off to a cross, we scrambled in the dirt, scooped the coins back into their boxes, and corralled the sheep back into their pens—sheep never go too far anyway.

And as you were crucified, we sold off more doves to the righteous, never wondering why people got so poor they could not afford to sacrifice an ox.

To the one who thought religion was to serve and not be served, we pray . . .

* Jesus cleansing the temple John 2:13-25

## NERVOUS RELATIVES*

Holy and merciful God, we thank thee for life, your Son Jesus, and even for this day. We are grateful for these days, Creator God, they pass and pass some more, and we think some other days passed too somewhere along the way while in quarantine. It is difficult to tell one day from the next sometimes; there are only so many shows to binge.

Only so many gallons of ice cream to eat before we wonder, was this our finest hour?

Or was it our worst?

What, O Lord, did you see within us as you gazed upon our lives in quarantine? Did you see our best or did you see our worst?

We give to you, O God of Dark and Light, all our days. The times we, by your Spirit, triumphed over stinginess and insult. And the times we, without your Spirit, caused a dose of misery to others.

Thank you for those we spend our days with; though they may get on our last nerve, you the Creator of our nervous system know ultimately salvation is a family affair and we do not get to pick our relatives.

We pray as Jesus taught us to pray . . .

---

* Prayer given during COVID quarantine

# NEW YEAR'S EVE 2020/21

Holy and Merciful God, you have brought many of us to the threshold of a new calendar year, and we are grateful. We pray and lament the ones who do not join us, there were a lot more than expected, even as we give thanks to you for their lives and for your charge over them unto this hour. For in your Son's life, death, and resurrection is hope not only for the dead but for the living.

God of all living flesh, we mark the passage of your time even as you live within it and outside of it as creator of it. We do wonder sometimes what time means, in light of relationship with you in eternity.

God of the Living and of the Dead, we are grateful for this year you have given us. We must say that pandemic was quite a surprise. We didn't see that one coming . . . did you?

God who seeks all lost people, perhaps this was not our finest year, perhaps we have not come out of this pandemic a better people, or a kinder people. Perhaps we will come out of it believing in science but not in you.

Perhaps we come out of this year with a clearer sense of our selfishness, our indifference to the elderly, our meanness to people of color, our separation from those without jobs or safe shelter.

God of a Jewish Covenant, perhaps this is a year where we must again ask permission to join your covenantal people, to give you, again, our consent . . . to be your servant and to tell the truth that you are our God, to follow your Son, who loves the dark and finds in it friendship.

In our gratefulness and in your Son's name we pray . . .

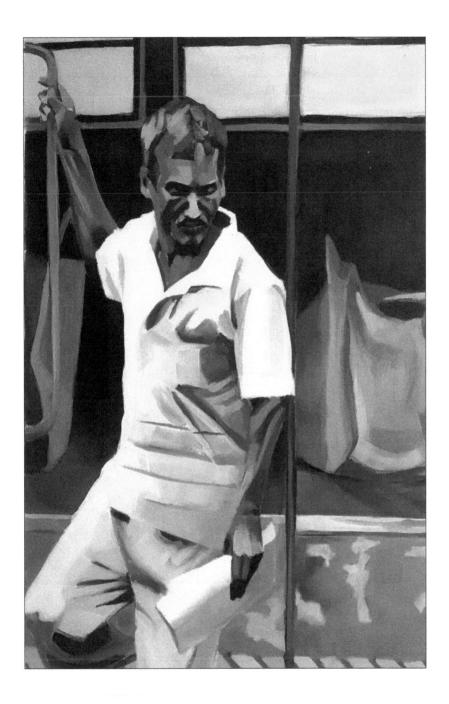

## NICELY RELIGIOUS

Holy and Merciful God, giver of saints and sinners alike, giver of redeemed and reprobates, we come to you this day thankful.

We pray for Kevin Peterson, a black man killed by police this past week. We pray for his family. We pray for the officers who killed him and will now live with his death the rest of their lives.

Jesus, if you could turn water into wine, then there is hope you can turn our sins and the sins of those we love and the sins of our enemies into something resembling the character of Christ.

To our Redeemer, by the Holy Spirit, we give to you the haughty in spirit, for you already have the poor ones.

We give to you the indifferent, for you already have those who mourn.

We give to you those who are arrogant, for you already have the meek.

To our Redeemer, by the Holy Spirit, we give to you those who couldn't care less about justice and righteousness, for you already have those who thirst and hunger for them.

We give to you the cruel, for you already have the merciful.

We give to you those who are selfish and self-centered, for you already have the pure in heart.

To our Redeemer, by the Holy Spirit, we give to you those who commit war and violence, for you already have the peacemakers.

We give to you those who abuse their power, for you already have the persecuted.

Jesus, it is not easy to be persecuted, reviled, and be a white middle-class American Christian. For we often mistake being polite for faith.

We sit protected most of the time by the powers of this world in all their cruelty. May the Holy Spirit move us to seek discipleship regardless of the cost, for there will rejoicing be found.

In the name of the one who was atrociously treated by really nice religious people we pray . . .

## OUTSIDE

Sheltering God, we pray for those without shelter. As you know, it went down below freezing last night, and we pray for those living outside — either by the choices they are making or by the cruelty others imposed upon them. We pray for those without an indoors to go to.

Holy Spirit, driven to the seams of civilization by addiction or mental illness or by preference or by the absence of friendship, by racism or by poverty or health, Holy Spirit we pray for those living outside.

Jesus Christ, they, our brothers and sisters, lay under cardboard boxes and damp blankets or tents and blue tarps, they perch precariously on the boundaries of our busyness as we cast our eyes on the future.

And you, Son of God, are like them, you lived a life where, unlike foxes in their dens and the birds in their nests, you also had nowhere to place your head.

Gracious God, Jesus told us you have a house with many rooms. How will you house the houseless? Will everyone have a room or will we have roommates?

You who had no room in the inn, how do we make a room, make room for those we do not know how to live with now?

We pray as Jesus taught us to pray . . .

## PALM SUNDAY

Holy and Merciful God, today, Palm Sunday, we recognize that your Son Jesus arrives in Jerusalem, the city that kills the prophets, arrives with happiness and joy, shouting, fanfare, and chaos. Hosanna! Later we will kill him with equal fanfare and relief, parades and what not. Hosanna!

We like to kill, O God, if not in your name, at least in our nation's. Murder occurs in all sorts of sizes, divine if you like extra-large, patriotic if you like the regular.

Gracious God, when Jesus shows up, desperate people jostle for a better position like 12-year-olds fawning over a boy band.

Why is it, Jesus, that we rarely see the dust of impending death surrounding our adoring idols, swirling unsettled around our hearts like mortal ash? Our methods of salvation are so far from yours.

Dear Jesus, there is no way to get from Palm Sunday to Easter without traveling across your back stretched out on two pieces of wood.

Holy Spirit, how do we put down our power in order to pick up your cross? How do we release our care for those we love? You placed our children, our parents, our siblings, our friends within our care. And now you would have us turn our heart from them to you . . . a donkey-riding soon-to-be-crucified messiah.

It is not much to go on. So this Sunday, we shout and wave but mostly we wait.

Hosanna!

Praying as you taught us to pray . . .

## PALM SUNDAY II

Holy and Merciful God, it is Palm Sunday and the people have gathered to usher you into Jerusalem.

God of marches, protests, and funeral processions, you always attract a crowd wherever you go. People notice you. They want to touch you and be close to you.

And they want to kill you.

You have that way about you, Jesus. Either people worship you or crucify you.

The tepid middle doesn't seem to work with you. And so, forgive us when we attempt lukewarm faith.

You require boldness, you sent a Son, a beloved member of the Trinity, God of Gods, Lord of hosts; to live with boldness, to die with innocence, to rise from the tomb of murder.

And you give us, this morning by the power of the Holy Spirt, a message to proclaim: That you, O God, will not stand apart. You, O Majesty beyond Majesties, will do the most human thing a person will do . . . die.

And we will hold the hammer and pound the nails.

And you know it.

And we know you know it, and yet we pound away anyway . . . any way we can.

If we can't reach your body, then we will reach for one of your own. The past two weeks we killed with a gun; a police officer, we killed grocery shoppers, we killed Asian-Americans, we killed husbands, and wives, spa workers* seeking a living, not death by gunfire.

* Mass shooting in Atlanta on March 16, 2021

We come to you because we have nowhere else to turn. With our praise and with our lament, who else would take us, O Lord? And who else has the power to strip us of our violence and transform our love of guns into our love of neighbor.

We pray this in the name of the one who died our death . . .

## PILLOW AND HAMMER

Holy and Merciful God, we thank thee for your Son Jesus Christ, and the fear-breaking power over death and sin he wields, and even for this day.

O Lord Jesus Christ, you come as a pillow and as a hammer. You softly smother the griping and stingy complaints of your disciples with talk of lost sons and lost coins, with downy images of yeast and flour, with little children and lilies of the field.

O Lord Jesus, you kick down the door of death and hades. You take your cross and wallop upon the spiritual forces of oppression, flinging them into a lake of fire till their dross of disobedience is burned off like fat on a rack of pork ribs . . . so that they can return in fellowship with you.

For "returning in fellowship with you" is your never-ending goal that through your Holy Spirit you pursue like a relentless cheetah taking down a gazelle.

For you refuse to end life until you have grabbed each little molecule of sin, each little hormone of greed and pride, each little chemical of violence, until you have drowned them and us underneath baptismal waters and we come up breaking the surface of heaven drenched in gratitude, because you will not, you will never not leave us alone.

Forgive us who are protected and safe to the point of boredom. There are so many of your people desperately scrambling for work, for a paycheck, for space, for heat, for food who could just use some wise compassion and we must, we absolutely must, give such compassion to them for there is no other way to follow you.

And now we pray to the wisest compassionate Christ we know . . .

## PLEASE SLOW DOWN

Jesus the Christ, it was you who became flesh, to live, to laugh, to suffer, to die, to be raised from the dead. You are not simply our pioneer going before us into your Kingdom, you are our perfecter making it possible for us to go along with you.

Jesus the Christ, please slow down, do not go so fast to your kingdom. We want to tarry and consider our options, we want to find the most appeasing gospel, one which allows us to enter the kingdom unburnt, undead, untouched . . . and thus unloved.

Jesus the Christ, you are not burdened by possessions and the concerns they bring. So please slow down and let us consider the lilies . . . and our money or lack of money.

Christ the King, lift us from our shame or from our pride, for you did not create us to be lost. Your kingdom was made not only in the shape of our hearts, but also by the shape of those we hate.

Through the power of the Holy Spirit, we pray for our enemies. It often took us no time at all to come to hate them, so it might take a lifetime to come to love them, which starts with desire, which starts with prayer, which starts with your grace, which starts with you.

Now we pray for that grace, as Jesus taught us to pray . . .

## PLEASURABLE WARS

We believe in the Holy Spirit, by this we mean, we need you Holy Spirit. We will remain mired in the tragedy of sin without your power to break its slick sick over our hands and speech.

We believe in Jesus Christ her son, by this we mean, we need you God-Man to become our idol before which all flaccid allegiances flee.

We believe in God, the Mother Almighty, the Father of Deep Sorrow, by this we mean we need you God of Sarah and Abraham more than we need our loved ones' safety.

We praise you, divine trinity: our Ghost, our Crucified, our Holy Intruder.

End our wars and the indifference and pleasure by which we fight them. End our scarcity and the way our souls are shaped by it. End our distraction and the fear by which we grasp it.

Bring us to enter the deep sound of your silence, where people are fed and refugees are embraced, and the only aliens are found in our science fiction, not the other side of our walls, and we discover that we were loved all along.

We pray as Jesus taught us to pray . . .

## POST-ELECTION*

Holy and Merciful God, we give you thanks that our country has, at this point, been able to endure another election. That you put up with us for these last 18 months is truly a sign of your mercy and goodness.

We grieve for those whose fear has increased, whose safety has decreased, who are in despair over the state of their neighbor's decisions and worry and worry and worry and worry.

Jesus, on Tuesday we did not get the collective exhale of relief we were looking for. So with cautious hearts, and hesitant words, and crossed fingers we ask you, did we make the world better?

Did we rearrange chairs on the pool deck of the local country club, or did we make it better for the least, the last, and the lost?

You tell us God, and we will listen. We stand before your judgment with bated breath. Seeking your compassion in need of your light.

Holy Spirit, we are no less divided than we were before Tuesday, and . . . we need our neighbors. So we give this contradiction to you. Only your reconciliation will work.

Holy Spirit, we pray for Jim. Before he was ours, he is yours. As you gave him to us for companionship, for friendship, for love, so we now give him back to you. May he rest in his labors in your presence till he is risen to join the saints at your heavenly banquet.

And now to the one who holds Jim and us and our country, we pray . . .

* Presidential Election November 2020

## PROFIT

To the One who underwent great suffering we pray. You ask us, Jesus, what will it profit us to gain the whole world and forfeit our lives? Why do you ask these questions of us? What would it profit us to gain the whole world?

A lot!!! Dear Jesus, we would profit a lot. There would be a lot of profit in gaining the whole world.

O One who went to great suffering for this world, leaving aside the part about losing our life, weren't we already going to lose that anyway?

If we gained the world, O One who left throne and glory, we could make a difference. If we gained the world we could clean up the place, make it into our own image. Why do you ask us these questions, O One who lost his life so that the world might be found?

Maybe we should ask questions back? Maybe that is what faith is? To believe One is worth questioning? What does losing our life look like, O One whose life returned from death? It sounds like we would be deeply lost from you, maybe irredeemably so, maybe not.

You, the One who exchanged your life for ours, this world is a suffering place, of that you know we are sure, for no one puts on skin and lives. You came not to suffer but to save. We made sure you suffered, for salvation is costly, if not for us then it certainly was for you.

Forgive us when we forget the death it cost . . . for us to live.

To the Resurrected Suffering Servant we pray . . .

## PROVERBS

Holy and Merciful God, we thank thee for life, love, and art. They remind us of creation and thus of you.

We pray for our earth. It does nothing but give its life to us as we do very little but take its life from it.

We pray for poets, for their subversive politics wrapped in velvet syllables.

We pray for those who pray. We just might make it into heaven riding on the backs of their offerings.

We pray for Donald Trump. He reminds us to vote.

We pray for the Kingdom of God. It will come without our votes.

We pray for the poor. They own the Kingdom of heaven, and no one gets in without their blessing.

We pray for the caretakers of the very young and the very old. One day we will need someone to hold our hands as we go potty.

We pray for farmers. They teach us how merciless you can be with weather – how helpless we are to rain and insects and fungus and heat and drought.

We pray for those living in cities who forget how much we need farmers.

We pray for writers and preachers, through words and The Word incarnate you have revealed yourself.

We pray for teachers, who teach us how to read in the first place.

We pray for those who mourn, they teach us to be silent.

We pray for businessmen, who make it possible to earn a living.

We pray for businesswomen, who do the same but for less pay.

We pray for marriages, they make us believe that commitments can last a lifetime. If we can love until death parts us, maybe even you God could love us—past death itself.

We pray as your Son Jesus taught us to pray . . .

## QUEER*

Dear God, this was an awful week for those of us who wanted a bigger, kinder, more vital church. One day we might learn, One day we might accept . . . last Tuesday was not that day, and we are sorry.

Jesus of the powerless, we took away a seat from your table. You invited the halt, the sick, and those who were too busy. You invited your children to sit with you, you invited your betrayers to break bread with you, you invited your servants to share a cup, and as we drank we became your friends.

You, Jesus, constantly invited, and healed, and brought to life, and reached out, and caressed, and cared for. How could we ever do the opposite?

We are sorry God. We failed to be an obedient church. We kept your children at a distance. We did one of the worst things a follower of yours could do. We chose safety.

Creator God, we the church are your Son's body. If we have done anything against the least of these, we have done it unto you. Today the least of these are our queer brothers and sisters—those who have been left out—those who were not allowed to experience completely the joys and sorrows of your church.

We did not invite them to be our pastors, we shouted down their call, we shut them away from their vocation, and we did not allow them to exchange their vows of love beside your altar. We deliberately took away their seat at your table.

Forgive us for all the decades of good they could have done within the title of Reverend but never did. Forgive us for all the covenants we could have blessed but didn't. It was as if we cut off a body part.

Having mauled your body once before, make us humble lest we do it again. We are especially mindful of those for whom rejection means more vulnerability to taking their own life.

* UMC General Conference's decision in February 2019 not to allow LGBTQ+ full inclusion

Jesus, the Prince of Peace, you always move towards forgiveness. You, O Resurrected One, returned on Easter not for vengeance but for friendship.

Indwell among us, Holy Spirit, as we the church stand against the very church we love.

## QUESTING*

Creator God, we thank you for your earth, the moon, and the stars that you have established. What are we in their presence?

Who do we think we are when standing in the night and the darkness of your universe, the dots of starlight suspended too far for us to reach?

God of Genesis, it is probably better that we do not touch another planet, having treated this one so poorly. And yet we cannot help but explore and push and hold. God of the Promised Land, you did this to us, you gave us yearning and restlessness so that we chaffed against the known landscape.

And so we seek, Dear God, we seek. May our questing always be accompanied by pondering. May our curiosity always come with contemplation. May we seek not so much to conquer as to share. And as we taste the apple of unknowing, may we do so not so much to acquire, as to revere.

Jesus, you are the master Gardener, with dirt underneath your nails and the mud of our existence still clinging to your britches. You breathed into us and created our life. So generous was your Holy Spirit within us that we could create meaning and purpose without you, without knowing you, without considering you.

May we tremble before your humility, O Lord. May we seek a generosity to match your own, such that the children of our enemies, that is your children, be considered as deeply as you consider our own.

We are all, after all, only creatures of your birthing, dependent upon your thin atmospheric membrane of love protecting us from the abyss of a howling darkness.

And so, as we strive for shelter under your wings we pray as Jesus taught us praying . . .

* Psalm 8

## RAIN

Holy and Merciful God, we thank thee for the gift of life, for your love, and even for this day.

We thank you for the rain, our patch of earth was thirsty. And we pray for those living outside who are now wetter and colder.

Creator God, your blessing often comes with mixed results. The rain gives life to our flora and fauna, and the rain brings chill and darkness to the vulnerable on our streets.

Holy Spirit, your actions in our world can be disarmingly tender and overwhelmingly grim often in the same breath you exhale.

Hurricanes blow and waters surge. You save some from danger and we have no choice but to offer thanksgiving. Others are killed and we have no choice but to cry.

Jesus, you call us to new life, but death is the doorway to get there. The rain falls indiscriminately on just and unjust alike.

God of covenant, you blessed Jacob, but Esau is left to bellow, "Have you not reserved a blessing for me?" Where, O Mothering God, are the blessings for the Esau's of this world? When do they get a chance to wrestle grace from your clenched lips?

And when will we ever stop . . . just stop . . . and listen to the sound of your sheer silence?

Perhaps we cannot hear you, until we say thank you, until you say you're welcome, until you say you are welcome into my creation, until we see Christ as the blessing you have reserved . . . for all.

Until we learn to live out the prayer Jesus taught us to pray . . .

## RAISING THE DEAD

Holy and Merciful God, we thank thee even for this day. We are especially mindful of Lori and her family upon her death. Comfort us in our grief as you welcome her into the joy of your resurrection.

Prodding, pushing, pushy God, you shove us into the world, to be you, to be your ambassador, your love made flesh, your blood and bone and heart muscle.

Resurrected Jesus, your Abba wants us to go into cities and towns raising the dead.* Who taught us to raise the dead? What words does one use to raise the dead? Jesus, I do not recall my Sunday School teachers mentioning we are to raise the dead. I think I would have paid better attention if they had.

Holy Spirit, you ignite us to cleanse the lepers and cast out demons and cure the sick. We pull weeds and cut the church grass each Thursday. Does that count?

Tell us what we are missing? Tell us, dear Jesus, what and how and where to begin?

You ask us God, to bring peace . . . could you be more specific? Did you mean peace between nations or in our hearts? What belongs to you and what belongs to Caesar? Are we splitting hairs, are we trying to hold something back from you?

This must be impossible . . . without you. It must be impossible without us.

We pray for you, for having to haul your Kingdom near . . . using us. It must be as aggravating for you as it is for us. Yet say the word and we will be made well.

We await, and as we wait, we pray the prayer you taught us . . .

* Matthew 10

109

## REPENT

O God, the one who blots our sins and purges with hyssop, the God of King David, and Bathsheba, and Uriah, and of that dead child that came out of David's abuse, for you must be a God of the most vulnerable.

As you know, O Redeemer, having been there, King David murdered a husband and stole his wife, abusing his power in all kinds of ways. We might have not done that, recently . . . or maybe we have, we don't mean to hide.

Our sins are ever before us. We assume they must be ever before you, as we assume you are interested in the same things we are interested in, our sins being one of them.

You do seem to be interested in telling the truth, so to you, our Redeemer, we tell the truth, we do bad things from time to time. And from time to time, we do not do good things that need to be done.

As a case in point, Dear Lord, when we get a bunch of us together and we form a less than perfect union we do some really bad things in order to keep national power and sovereignty.

Why, sometimes our allegiance to country is more important to us than our allegiance to your Son.

And we have addictions and habits of hardness that drive this earth to the brink of extinction and our relationships to the brink of dissolution.

And, Creator God, if ever there was a year to tell the truth that we are mortal this would be the year, what with the pandemic and all. We are heading for the grave or urn or sprinkled on a mountain or however a body that is a little lower than God is to be cared for.

We are not the best at creatureliness. At least a tree doesn't sin, or a racoon, or a swan. So, let us take a moment in your presence, O Lord, to tell the truth about our sins and mortality and seek the power to repent . . . Resurrected Christ, to you we give thanks. Amen

## REST

O Holy and Merciful God, we thank thee for your Son our Savior, your Spirit our life, and even for this day.

God of Genesis, we pray for rest. Not quarantine, not monotony, not isolation, but sabbath. A laying down of the things our minds like to pick up and fret over, a laying down of the things our sin-sick souls use to forget you are God and we are not.

Yet if you grant us rest, O Holy Spirit, let us rest like you rested during the great creation, when you spun off giraffes and elephants like a spider spinning off silk, when you spawned off mountains and oceans like chinook salmon spawning eggs in November.

Do not let us rest like the disciples who could not keep their eyes open in the garden when Jesus was in need. Do not let us rest if rest means closing our eyes to the cry for friendship. Give us no rest from race hatred and white privilege and monied politics.

If you grant us rest let us rest like a farmer eating lunch under a tree munching soundlessly as she contemplates the work ahead.

Let us rest like a violinist between movements, flexing her hands

Let us rest like Usain Bolt after the semi-finals with one more win to go.

Let us rest like a cancer patient between chemo, seeking solace just breathing, just breathing, responsible for the present moment and no more

Let us rest because we got stunned by the color of a bush, or the flatness of a salt desert, or the smoothness of a pool before jumping in—or because your Son went off to pray, before he went off to die.

The kind of rest to remember we are not in charge. The kind of rest that trusts you to take care of things while we close our eyes to breathe just breathe.

As your sabbath teacher Jesus Christ taught us to pray . . .

## RESTORE OUR FORTUNES*

Holy and Merciful God, we thank thee for your Son, the source of our salvation, and we thank thee for the Holy Spirit, the power of our existence.

Restore our fortunes, O Lord, just like the Psalm tells us.† Restore our fortunes, O Lord. But by *our* we also mean the fortunes of all citizens of the land, strangers, migrants, all war-torn refugees, economic outcasts, those running away from gang violence. All those who never had fortunes to begin with.

Restore our fortunes, O Lord, be they fortunes of friendship or love, fortunes of the heart or home.

But do not restore our fortunes, O Lord, if it means adding to our distractions. Or if it means taking from the fortunes of others. Our sin-sick souls cannot handle any more wealth.

And we hate to say this, O Lord, but restore the fortunes of our enemies. You know who they are, Lord, for we hold them close to our hearts and imaginations. Sometimes we give them greater dominion than we give you. Forgive us.

And if we cannot pray for our enemies, O Lord, then at least give us the power to pray for the children of our enemies.

And if we refuse to pray for the children of our enemies, then do with us what you must, until our identity is grounded in you and not our pain.

As those with fortunes or those without, we pray as Jesus taught us to pray . . .

* This prayer was influenced by the work of Garret Keizer
† Psalm 126

## SAFE IDOLATRY

Holy and Merciful God, we thank you for your Son, our Savior and Lord, born into danger, that is, born into this world. And we thank you even for this day.

Gracious God, we are unsure what to do, for there is violence around us and sometimes within us. We see violence in the streets, we hear violent rhetoric in speeches, we see the violent breakdown of bodies to an invisible virus, we even see violence in nature. We entertain violence in our thoughts and words even as we are entertained by violence in our distractions.

Most of us just watch it all while others tell us what to think and do and we ponder how we can stay safe.

What does it mean to worship you, O Son of the Living God? What does it mean to worship you and seek safety at the same time? You who warned us of the dangers of following you, as you went out to the streets touching lepers and getting in trouble with authorities for touching lepers, as if touching the least, the last, and the lost were threatening.

Son of David, Son of Mary, what did you go out on the streets for, you who warned us that we would be dragged to court and beaten and rejected by our own families for following you?*

Really what kind of God are you that you do not protect us like we think you should?

What could possibly be more important to you than our own safety? Unless our safety has become a form of worship itself? Our safety becomes idolatry.

And so, as with all our idols, we bring them before you, O God who purges and cleanses and judges and calls and sends out again. For we ask once again to cleanse our hearts . . . point us to right worship.

Let us pray as Jesus taught us . . .

* Luke 21

114

# SAINTS*

Dear Lord Jesus, Creator and Sustainer – this day we come before you with gratitude for our saints. For the saints in our life who have passed on faith; faith to you, faith for you, faith in you.

And we pray for the saints who have passed on to us doubt, uncertainty, anger in the face of suffering, and the assurance that misgivings and bald face indictment against you are part and parcel of Christian faith.

Dear Lord Jesus, this day we come before you thankful for the saints of the church, which include those who never went to church, but loved us into faith anyway, the parents who dropped us off at the church door each week and drove away with some vestige of faith ringing ever so quietly in their ears, their duty done.

Dear Lord Jesus, we thank you for the saints who taught us, and sung us, and prayed us, and fed us, and confronted us, and loved us, into some kind of faith where we would, more often than not, show up to your church seeking some good news.

Dear Lord Jesus, we thank you for saints who walked with us beside still waters and troubled waters, who laid down with us in green pastures of abundance and barren deserts of disbelief, the saints who whacked us with their staff to get us out of self-absorption, and yes, those saints who did not run away when we walked through the death valley of shadows.

Dear Lord Jesus, we thank you for saints, who prepared us to sit at our enemy's table, and experience the balm of forgiveness and the cup of reconciliation. The saints who have gone before us with goodness and mercy, whether we remember them or not.

Dear Lord Jesus thank you for saints, may they dwell in your home forever. We pray as the Saint Maker taught us to pray . . .

* All Saint's Sunday

116

## SAUCY BOLDNESS

O Christ whose body born lash and spike, O Christ who rose from ash and dirt, O Christ who hauled yourself out of the grave dusting off the palms of your nail-scarred hands like you did nothing but a little housecleaning and laundry, to you we offer praise, praise, and 1000 praises again.

For you have done for creation what you as Creator intended to do all along.

O Resurrected Jesus, the end was always Easter, the goal was an empty tomb, the plan was death defeated, the mission was sin forgiven, the purpose was new life.

And now we have seen the End, and it is good.

Easter is not your response to a world gone awry; Easter is your revelation that our awried world orbits your love.

And now, now we can laugh and now we can sing and now we can face the future unafraid. Armed with your resurrected power, we can dive deep into the chaos and violence of earth hatred and race hatred and gender hatred all the many hatreds which pretend that death is king.

And in the name of Jesus Christ, we declare, "Hatred, you are dethroned, for Christ is Lord, Christ has died, Christ is risen, Christ will come again."

In saucy boldness we pray . . .

## SCATTERED SMATTERED AND SMOTHERED

Gracious God, we come before you scattered, smattered, and smothered by our loves and losses, by our worries and distractions, by our needs and by our desires.

We scramble for everything but kindness, we search for all but compassion, we forgot to care for the poor, the houseless, the addicted, the imprisoned, for that sister who cheated us, for the uncle who hurt us, for the friend who betrayed us, for the enemy that killed us . . .

Forgive us Holy Spirit, our trespasses, but not like we forgot to forgive those who trespassed against us. Rather forgive us like Jesus would. Like Jesus would on a day when he was moved with tenderness. But not like a day when he was angry, not that kind of day. Rather forgive us dear Jesus on a day when you were moved with pity.

May we remember you as the sole author of life. In the end all memory of hell of whatever form will cease, all friction will be calmed, all hate will be removed, all hunger will be banished, all storms will be stilled, all the rough edges of our heart will be made smooth.

You, Lord Jesus, became human and lived in solidarity with us, for you lived our lives, loved our affections, journeyed our fate, died our death, and rose from the dead as our pioneer, the first through the breach beyond where death has no dominion and only your love reigns.

We pray as Jesus our Savior taught us to pray . . .

## SEMEN AND EGG*

Gracious God, this morning we hear the Good News that a prophet, John the Baptist, has been/will be born.

Wording God of Scripture, you give us an odd story about a forlorn and faithful couple.

Thank you for Zechariah and Elizabeth, that we may emulate their piety without rancor. Thank you for priests and barren women; we look forward to the day when women will be priests and men will be less fertile.

Birthing God, thank you for terrifying scaly angels with upsetting news of a quirky birth. We believe, O God, that you are such an odd God for connecting gynecology with salvation.

For in our little world today we connect salvation with military might and violent power, but you O Holy Spirit . . . you bring about the transformation of the world with semen and egg and a uterus . . . how strange.

Jesus of those in half-way houses, orphanages, foster homes, adoption centers; Jesus of couples and singles who hope for new birth and yet experience dreams deferred; who have experienced still births, abortions, fertility clinics, poking and prodding, and examinations and conclusions.

May we know the peace and quiet of your mothering healing womb encompassing your creation; encompassing us and our enemies. You, Holy Spirit, fussing over us, waiting to see what we may create, and who we may be, and hoping we will get out of the way in time.

Let's us pray a prayer of expectation as Jesus taught us praying . . .

* Luke 1

## *SILENTLY*

Gracious God, in Christ Jesus your Son we find your love. Or maybe Christ Jesus's love finds us. It is a love that sustains us as quietly as the air moving in our chest, as necessary as breath. If we did not notice we would have missed it completely.

Holy Spirit, you bring us the love of Christ, at times boldly, convincingly, unabashedly, even intrusively.

But mostly silently, if we were completely honest about it, mostly silently does your love come, to be honest. Which of course is the only way to pray about these matters . . . that is, with honesty.

Lord Jesus, during those times when we were not honest about your love, when we forgot it existed or when we used it to become self-righteous . . . forgive us.

Forgive us even as we hold you accountable to your promises. For starters, the promise to be with us to the ends of the earth.

Which is why we pray. To be with you to the ends of our earth.

Which is why we pray . . .

## SMELL LIKE US

Holy and Merciful God, we thank thee for this day, for life and love, and the coming of your Son into this world.

We lift up to you Denise and Ron. Before they were ours they are yours. Comfort us in our grief, even as we proclaim the sure and certain hope found in Christ's resurrection conquering sin and death.

Jesus, Son of God and Son of us all, may we not only be inspired by you, but may we love as you love.

Jesus, you show us that love costs our lives but the alternative is death.

Spirit of God, do not forgive us our power, but do forgive our fear of power, for it leads to bad leaders.

Spirit of God, we do not ask for forgiveness for our loves, but we do seek forgiveness for the way our loves did not transcend our family, our political parties, our country, our race, our earth killing way of life.

Spirit of God, we do not ask for forgiveness for our biases but for directing them towards the clean and against the addicted, towards the Americans and not the Mexicans, towards those who smell like we do, who vote like we vote, who own the same as we own.

Gracious God, we will always hate, but force us to hate what brings death, not those who bring it. To hate the dominion of death, not those possessed by it. To hate violence not those who perpetrate it.

And then by your return, force us to hope that one day you will put an end to those things which bring division: nationalism, racism, and greed among them.

As we hope we pray as Jesus taught us praying . . .

## SPRING GRADUATION

Gracious God, we thank you for all those graduating this spring. Regardless of what they are graduating from – from addiction, from pre-school, from greed, from Harvard, all those who have moved to something different, who have finished a goal, completed a stage, accomplished something good. We thank you for the way your grace has been shaped in their lives.

Heavenly Mother, we humbly offer to you that any work we do, any accomplishment we secure, is a result of your pregnant love, whether acknowledged or not. We participate in your kingdom to come, we do not create it out of our own efforts.

Thank you, Holy Spirit, for the resiliency it took to graduate. For some it meant grit and hard work, for others it simply meant showing up on a fairly consistent basis.

Jesus, walk with us in our nervousness about what comes next. Give us hope that the same God who is present in the future is the same one who gutted it out next to us in our past.

You are the God of Abraham and Sarah, Rebekah and Isaac, Rachel and Jacob, and Leah, also Bilhah, and let's not forget Zilpah. You walked with our ancestors through much worse than we will mostly walk in our lifetime.

Through your power may we hold on to faith like the way snow hangs on to Mt. Hood in summer, clinging in the dark crevasses with tenacity until October rains.

In Jesus's name we pray . . .

## *STUFF*

Gracious God, thank you for our stuff. We have a lot of it, and we appreciate it. If we got our stuff because others didn't get any stuff . . . we are sorry.

If, in making our stuff for us, it meant others didn't have health insurance or a livable wage or workers' compensation or treated with dignity . . . we are sorry.

Forgive us for living as if our stuff was the source of life. Forgive us for squandering your precious gift of life to get more stuff. We were only trying to provide for ourselves and for those we love. We were only trying to find the goodness of work.

Remind us that working is necessary and meaningful, but that greed is a cold lifeless god.

Forgive us when, by giving our stuff to others, we made it worse. We were only trying to be compassionate.

Bless us O God, when we gave some of our stuff to others and it helped them to know compassion, or by sharing our stuff, others thrived

Teach us to pray as Jesus taught us praying . . .

## TALL WAVES*

Holy and Merciful God, Usherer of new life, Bringer of glad tidings, Resplendent Radiant Blackness, Author of stars and solar flares, Founder of zygotes and brown thrushes, Inaugurator of inaugurations, the King Maker of kings.

To you we pledge our hopes and fears and loves. To you we give our praise and what little glory we could muster this morning behind our phones, computer screens, and TV sets.

So quickly take them—our hopes, fears and loves. Take them or else we will fritter them away before lunchtime. You created us so there is much that is lovely about us, and we forget that our loveliness originates in you.

This forgetting gets us into all kinds of trouble.

Like Jonah, we'd rather get swallowed by an Orca than proclaim peace to the Ninevites, or was it the Iranians, or was it the Trumplicans, or was it the Democrats?

We would rather get pitched off a ship than put on a mask for our neighbor. We would rather die in a sea storm than confront our own racism.

Lord, our common life is a mess. We got rid of one president only to replace with another. Neither one strong enough to keep us from hatred, though both strong enough to foment it. Neither one strong enough to check our self-interests . . .

So we look at the size of the waves and whether the sails are holding up and take our chances with the whales, preferring our detestations to our neighbor's salvation.

In the name of the one who swallows sinners and spits out supplicants we pray . . .

* January 2021

126

## TEACH US

Holy and Merciful God, we thank thee for the gift of your Son, your Spirit, and even for this day.

God of Genesis and Revelation—Beginning and End – Of Alpha and Omega, our lives are lived within the shadow of our death. May this give us the wisdom to share, since our grasping and clawing and clutching will come to an end anyway. We might as well practice opening our hands now.

Teach us to caress but not to cling.

Teach us to receive without hoarding.

Teach us to notice how others are doing and to engage in the work of their welfare.

Teach those who are white to stop and listen.

Teach those who are not to claim their identity as children of God.

Teach us all to pay attention to our planet. She appears to be rather angry and in great distress. Teach us to pray as Jesus taught us praying . . .

## TO BE YOU

Holy and Merciful God, we thank thee for your misunderstood Son, mislabeled Holy Spirit, and even for this day.

Jesus, what is it like to be you?

Is it like a black woman being ignored? Is it like a black man pulled over on a pretext? What is it like to be you? Is it like a migrant working through COVID? An Asian American being pushed to the ground? Is it like a shop owner closing down her business? A woman being assaulted? An addict with an infection? A Jew being persecuted?

Is it like the loneliness of someone who is mentally ill or the permanency of being poor? Can we slide in and out of being the last—one day powerless, the next day powerful? One day in the front and the next day in the back?

Jesus, who are you today? Who are the last of these through which our compassion or our thoughtless malevolence is also done unto you? We didn't mean to be mean; we were simply preoccupied.

Holy Spirit, what does it mean to blaspheme you? Does it mean giving up? Is it having faith in the goodness of people rather than in the triumph of your dominion? Or does it happen when we ignore the power of the persecuted? Is it mistaking the Messiah for Satan or declaring the Spirit unclean?

Christ, how do we become you in the world? Your Body in the world – your mother, your brother, your sister—not to be persecuted but to be in love.*

Three in One; Gracious God, last-of-these-Jesus, and profaned Spirit, please walk beside us, showing us your Word, until one day we put aside our shame, our complicit quietism, and do the will of God.

We pray as Jesus taught us to pray . . .

* Mark 3:20-35

## TO PRAY LIKE MARY

Holy and Merciful God, we thank thee for life, and love, the gift of your son, and even for this day.

Thank you for Marty and Cal, your children, before they were ours, they are yours. Comfort us in our grief as they await the sure and certain hope of resurrection.

Coming-apart-God, you give us your servant Mary, the mother of Christ. And you give her a voice to pray. And boy does she pray. She prays like the coming Christ has stomach churned a new kingdom into existence.

Birthing God, she prays like the right-side-up we assume must be, is exactly upside-down from the way God intended and will make it.

Dismantling God, she prays that those who are first will be last. That those who shout, "America First", should know they pray against the mother of God.

Teach us to pray like her!

New Life God, she prays for the powerful to be pulled down like confederate statues.

Converting God, she prays like the boasting and prideful will be scattered and smattered like hash browns at a Waffle House; your Holy Spirit blowing into empire, and First World dominance.

Teach us to pray like her!

Converting God, Mary claims that the powerful will be thrown down, but how do we throw down the powerful without violence?

Doesn't that make us powerful too?

Creating Holy Spirit, who are the powerful people? Is Donald Trump a powerful person? O Crucified One, should we throw him down?

Would we have joy in throwing him down or retributive violence? After all we are the ones who impale our enemies on crosses . . . not you.

Is there a difference between us doing the throwing or you? Does Mary testify to your strength or her own?

God of all, you come to us as a baby wrapped in vulnerable love . . . so who has the power?

Is your prayer powerful? To the one we pray as Jesus taught us to pray . . .

## TRANSFIGURATION

Holy and Merciful God, we thank you for your Son who went first through the breach of death and for your Holy Spirit who yanked him back.

We pray for your daughter Sally, in sure and certain hope of her bodily resurrection. Comfort us in our grief as we wait to eat together at a table large enough for all sinners and saints alike. Make Sally fit for the Kingdom of God as you receive her into the arms of your mercy.

Holy God, this morning we celebrate your Son's transfiguration on the top of a mountain. He went up to be glorified, he came down to be crucified. In between, he walked a road of rock and dust as your beloved toward a city that would kill him and a people who would betray him.

Thank you, God, for mountains, they are grand and beautiful and provide epiphanies and theophanies, and inspiration, and when we climb them, we take selfies, and feel like we have accomplished something.

We love our mountains, we summit them, we paint them, in West Virginia we blow the top off them to get coal.

We see them as things to be used. In your Holy Word you see them as a place where holiness is encountered, where the projects of humankind are silenced.

For all the crazy revelations you gave us on mountains, like stone tablets and white-faced prophets, the best had to be your Son our Savior. And so, we are thankful.

To the one who came off the mountain we pray . . .

## TUMMY RUBS

Holy and Merciful God, we thank thee for the gift of life, for this fragile and abundant earth, and for the gift of friendship.

God of lost souls, lost loves, and those who have lost their way.

God of lost lives, lost kids, lost hopes, and lost dreams.

Bless us in our need to be found, to have the rock under which we have hidden rolled away revealing your face looking at us the way a child finds a parent in a game of hide-and-seek.

O God, look at us like the way a dog looks at a returning owner. Quivering with anticipation seeking that first belly rub, waiting as we kick off our work shoes, the only labor ahead is one of furry tummies and touch.

Seek us until our funeral clothes are folded neatly and put away.

Seek us like a lover, seek us because we will never be found—until you brush our hair back and gaze at us until we stop squirming, hold still, and look back, which means you will gaze at us through wood and splinters and spikes and spittle, until all pain has pierced your flesh, until you say enough . . . we are finished with death.

Seek us not by our worth and work but by your exasperation, your begrudging eye rolling consent.

Seek us until we pray as Jesus taught us . . .

## UN-BOW OUR FACES

Holy and Merciful God, we thank thee for the beauty of the earth, it reminds us that we are mortal and dependent and powerful and weak all at the same time.

Creator God, we are made of the earth and to the earth we shall return, if not today then someday soon. With such a connection to our earth one would think we would take better care of it. The dark dirt is mixed, after all, with the dead bodies of our ancestors.

Your planet, like your Son, is a gift. Forgive us for pretending we earned it. We may be loved but no more so than anybody else we share this planet with. Teach us that to share this planet means just that . . . to share.

We cannot create out of nothing. We can only steward the elements and building blocks you first breathed out of your being.

Gracious God, give us awe over your cosmos, do not let us lose amazement, tilt our heads upwards away from our technology, un-bow our faces, hovered over our screens, so that we may cast our gaze upon the heavens and wonder where you live.

Keep us outside, make us to till the earth and plant a garden or lie in a field, or sit in the sun, or watch a cloud, or pitch a tent, or look at a bird, or pause from hard work to be still and know that you are God.

To Jesus, the divine earth dweller whose faith saves us all we pray as he taught us to pray . . .

## VETERANS

Holy and Merciful God, we thank thee for your Son—for in his life, death, and resurrection we find a hope that sticks like stew on a grey drizzling day.

Thank you, God, for the rain. We do not know how to have a fall without it.

Thank you, liberating God, for peace—if not on the earth, at least in our country, if not in our country at least in our families, if not in our families at least in ourselves, if not in ourselves at least within you.

Ever present Christ, if we cannot find peace within ourselves, then at the very least let us not inflict our conflict upon others.

O Crucified Christ, this Veteran's Day may we seek peace so that no child of yours will ever be called upon to kill some other child of yours.

Healing God, we pray for those Vets who are so spiritually broken they have separated themselves from you or have become lost from you for you never become lost from them. You hold them, you love them, you seek their return.

We pray for healing from PTSD that comes with the trauma of being injured, or from killing or injuring other human beings.

For those who have sought solace in opioids, alcohol, or have been cast into poverty, or houselessness, you are the great physician who knits us all back to health. Give us the power to accompany the wounded and weary, the tired and trampled upon. We pray as Jesus taught us to pray . . .

## WE ARE LONELY

Holy and Merciful God, we thank thee for our lives, your love, and even for this day. Out of this abundance may we go and serve the world.

Gracious God, we pray for people who are lonely. They may be surrounded by others or spend much of their days by themselves. They may be lonely because of decisions they made in times past or lonely because of hurt inflicted upon them.

Regardless, we pray for people who are lonely.

God in relationship, God three persons in one, God of trinity, never alone, never lonely, heavenly hosts constantly adoring you, well . . . except that one time in a garden, where you prayed for the cup of suffering to be taken away and it wasn't . . . and that other time on a cross, where you were forsaken, at least you said you were, and we depend upon you to tell the truth.

Forsaken Christ, perhaps you know what it is to ponder in unsolicited silence while the phone stays quiet and no one comes to your door.

We pray for people who are lonely.

Perhaps, dear Christ, that is why you went to so many parties. We are sorry for the times we left you alone when you wanted friendship.

Spirit of Holiness, we pray for company to come into our lives. The kind of company we anticipate with joy, the kind of company that keeps us checking the windows for their arrival.

The kind of company that brings greetings and cold dinner rolls from far off, the kind where we bounce to the door and hold it open letting the cold air in, while the dog gets out, and the hugs begin as we shout at the dog.

Dear God, give us company, the kind of company you ask of us.

To the one who knows our loneliness and traverses across death itself to banish it . . . we pray . . .

## WIND

Gracious God, we are told that you overcame chaos by breathing upon the dark matter of creation, blowing light and life into existence. You lifted Adam's dirty nose and breathed into it moisture for life to sprout.

With Moses, you split the Red Sea by wind, making a path for your children to flee slavery.

You blew apart the mountains and rocks to show Elijah your magnificent silence.

Your Son Jesus blew the Holy Spirit upon the church and birthed an earth-shattering movement.

So God, what are we to make of the winds not of Yahweh, Jesus, or Holy Spirit, but of Michael, Florence, and Harvey? *

You mysterious Lord, who are so comfortable with wind. What are we to make of winds that bring life and winds that kill?

Creator God, did your winds fall from grace along with your people? Did the winds get banished from the garden along with Eve and Adam; banished to stalk the earth?

Are winds alive, do they move, and do they sin? Do they, like us, flee from your heart and will, only to come back again and again?

Your winds move seeds to give food to feed a world. They moved commerce and trade for millennia. We harness the earth's breath for energy. Your wind is the source of our life, we breathe out music and speech and are dead without it.

Yet they also blew the soil and created a dust bowl of depression on the great plains and blow tornados across those same flat stretches.

* This prayer was written following three destructive hurricanes which ran aground in the United States in 2017 and 2018.

Almighty God, what are we to make of wind? Are they spirits of good or of evil? Can your creatures be both, at the same time? The membrane between good and evil is as close as one breath to the next.

Give us your power, O God, to take care of the victims of wind. And give us pause before we attribute their source or label their worth.

Most of all give us humility for we control nothing.

Give us over to pray as Jesus taught us praying . . .

## YOU WITHOUT IT

All Holy and Merciful God, we thank thee, even for this day.

Thank you, Lord Jesus, for standing among us and telling us the truth.

You show us your pain, without causing more of it.

You reveal your wounds, without injuring your world.

You walked through Good Friday, while standing firmly in Easter.

You overcome death, without taking away life.

You teach us our betrayal, while offering us forgiveness.

You display our violence, while bestowing upon us your peace.

You were brutalized by retribution, while calling us to reconcile.

You move us to serve, you shape our joy, you give us your love.

By the power of The Holy Spirit may we do likewise.

Now let us pray as Jesus taught us praying . . .

## YOUNG AND OLD

Gracious God, we lift up to you our children. The shy, the introverted, the autistic, the gifted, the not-so-gifted, the quiet ones, the obstinate ones, the down syndrome kids, the gay, the straight, the crooked, all who don't seem to fit in the square holes or the round holes either. May the diversity of humanity point out a characteristic of yours rather than give rise to prejudice of ours.

We include O Lord, the neglected kids, the abused ones, the ones we shut up with pixels, keep quiet with technology, and raise with pharmaceuticals. Teach us that your creatures are your beloved made in your image and are to be treated as such.

Gracious God, we lift up to you our elderly, the ones who have become invisible through no fault of their own. The elderly ones rendered irrelevant and transparent because we will not employ them or cannot commodify them anymore.

The elderly, Lord, the ones we ignore, except when we want money. The neglected elderly, the abused ones, the ones we shut up with pixels, keep quiet with technology, and pacify with pharmaceuticals. Teach us that your creatures are your beloved made in your image and are to be treated as such.

And most difficult of all, dear lord, so difficult we cannot possibly pray this without your grace . . . we pray for the children and the elderly of our enemies. We humbly know that we might stop hating our enemies when we must pray for their loved ones . . . we are willing to take the risk of having to let go of our hatred.

O God, we fearfully understand that you chose us, and yet you chose us not so we can bully the rest of the world, but so that we might bear witness to your sacrificial love for all your creation. And so, we pray as Jesus taught us praying . . .

# About the Author

ANDY OLIVER is a United Methodist pastor serving in Portland Oregon. As a minister he can rarely escape requests to pray and is often in search of words. Through graduate work at Anabaptist Mennonite Biblical Seminary, he has been heavily influenced to explore themes of violence and peace through congregational prayers. He holds an M.Div from Candler School of Theology at Emory University.

# About the Artist

RYAN HUTCHISON is an artist with a lifelong fascination with the human form and existence. He is a member of the church where Andy pastors. Ryan is also a primary care doctor working in a prison for adolescent boys, as well as a husband and a father to teenage children.